Praise for *Touching*

"*Touching This Leviathan* is many books а
book of faith, a book of teaching, a praxis or rhetoric, a ceto-bibliophile's
catalog of whaling arcana, a guide to the allure and disgust of flensing, and
the list could easily go on. But this undefinable something is itself part
of the book's deep charm, evidence of what it is to live in search of the
mysteries one is also next to."
  —Dan Beachy-Quick, author of *A Whaler's Dictionary*

"*Touching This Leviathan* is both memoir and meditation, exploring what it
means to watch and wait for whales, to live inside a whale, to flense a dead
whale, to use the word *whale*. Peter Moe's rich, thoughtful prose veers from
personal experiences to history and science while reading like epic poetry."
  —Erich Hoyt, research fellow, Whale and Dolphin Conservation,
    and author of *Orca: The Whale Called Killer*; *Insect Lives*; and
    Creatures of the Deep

"From citizen science to theology, from ecocriticism to writing theory,
from biological regionalism to literary criticism, Peter Moe's accomplished
interdisciplinary reach matches his firm grasp in this diverse and
fascinating book."
  —Paul Lindholdt, author of *Explorations in Ecocriticism: Advocacy,
    Bioregionalism, and Visual Design*

"In *Touching This Leviathan*, Peter Moe explores what it means to truly
know whales, deftly weaving together literary, biblical, and intimately
personal threads into a tapestry that invited me to see the majestic and
mysterious creatures I study with new eyes."
  —Ryan M. Bebej, biologist and paleontologist, Calvin University

TOUCHING THIS LEVIATHAN

The John and Shirley Byrne Fund for Books on Nature and the Environment provides generous support that helps make publication of this and other Oregon State
University Press books possible.

Dan Albergotti, "Things to Do in the Belly of the Beast" from *The Boatloads*.
    Copyright © 2008 by Dan Albergotti. Reprinted with the permission of
    The PermissionsCompany, LLC on behalf of BOA Editions, Ltd., boaeditions.org.
Lines from "My Life" from *The Nerve of It: Poems Selected and New* by Lynn
    Emanuel, © 2015. Reprinted by permission of the University of Pittsburgh Press.
Lines from "Choosing a Name" in *Collected Poems* by Anne Ridler, © 1995.
    Reprinted by kind permission of Carcanet Press.
Lines from "Swallowed Up (In The Belly Of The Whale)" by Bruce
    Springsteen. Copyright © 2012 Bruce Springsteen (Global Music Rights).
    Reprinted by permission. International copyright secured. All rights reserved.
The book includes excerpts from the author's work previously published in the
    following publications:
"Of Chiasms and Composition, or, The Whale, Part II." *Reader: Essays in Reader-
    Oriented Theory, Criticism, and Pedagogy* 65/66 (fall 2013/spring 2014): 88–107.
"Sounding the Depths of the Whale." *ISLE: Interdisciplinary Studies in Literature
    and Environment* 21, no. 4 (autumn 2014): 858–872.
"Of Tombs and Wombs, or, The Whale, Part III." *Leviathan: A Journal of Melville
    Studies* 17, no. 1 (March 2015): 41–60.
"Life after Death: How to Build a Whale." *Out There Outdoors*, June 2018, p. 44.
    outthereoutdoors.com/life-after-death-how-to-build-a-whale.
"Virginia Tufte's Sentences." *Style* 52, no. 4 (October 2018): 385–403.
A version of chapter 6, "To Flense," appeared in *Fourth Genre: Explorations in
    Nonfiction* 22, no. 2 (fall 2020): 35–48.

Cataloging-in-Publication Data

Names: Moe, Peter Wayne, author.
Title: Touching this leviathan / Peter Wayne Moe.
Description: Corvallis : Oregon State University Press, [2021] | Includes
    bibliographical references.
Identifiers: LCCN 2020057161 | ISBN 9780870713071 (trade paperback) |
    ISBN 9780870713101 (ebook)
Subjects: LCSH: Whales. | Whaling—Environmental aspects.
Classification: LCC QL795.W5 M58 2021 | DDC 599.5—dc23
LC record available at https://lccn.loc.gov/2020057161

♾ This paper meets the requirements of ANSI/NISO Z39.48-1992
(Permanence of Paper).

© 2021 Peter Wayne Moe
All rights reserved.
First published in 2021 by Oregon State University Press
Printed in the United States of America

Oregon State University Press
121 The Valley Library
Corvallis OR 97331-4501
541-737-3166 • fax 541-737-3170
www.osupress.oregonstate.edu

for our son

Contents

On Method

Touching This Leviathan asks how we might come to know the
unknowable—in this case, whales, animals so large yet so elusive,
revealing just a sliver of back, a glimpse of a fluke, or, if you're lucky
(and I rarely am), a split-second breach before diving away.

For me, this work of knowing is a problem of language, a problem
of how someone might locate the self within and against the sentences of others. And so I must read widely, promiscuously even.
Touching This Leviathan is necessarily interdisciplinary, looking to
biology, theology, natural history, literature, and writing studies.
I read not so that I can contribute to each of these fields but so that
they may, together, point me toward the whale.

In this book-length essay, I take a cue from Melville: "There
are some enterprises in which a careful disorderliness is the true
method." I employ this careful disorderliness, my project defined by
gathering extracts, by curating an archive. Key to the method, then,
are section breaks within each chapter. These jumps are an effort to
pull from as many places as possible, places perhaps not the most
obvious when trying to write the whale. With each jump, I take the
advice of Verlyn Klinkenborg: "Imagine a reader you can trust." I invite readers to piece together these sundry parts, this work mirroring
my own as we move, together, into the belly of the whale.

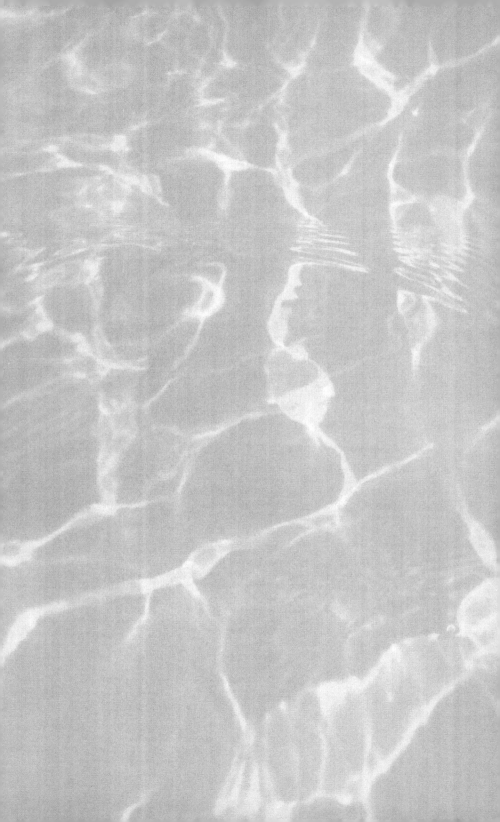

ONE } Knowing Beans

I know him not, and never will.
—Ishmael,
in Herman Melville's *Moby-Dick*

Because of wind and swells, I have little chance of seeing the misty spout of a gray whale. I'm on a beam reach off Santa Barbara. After three hours our captain spots something on the horizon. He brings the boat into the wind. Dolphins swim off our bow, and we gain on what looks to be a gray. Should the whale dive we'll lose it.

We arrive where the gray was sighted. The crew lowers the main and silent we wait. Moments later the whale surfaces parallel to our ship, ten feet off starboard. Its exhale sends me stumbling across the deck. Having only ever seen photographs of whales, I'm not prepared for the power (and stench) of its breath. Though I know better—unprovoked whales do not attack (or so I'm told; I hesitate to make any blanket statements about whales)—I find myself wondering what an animal that creates such force through merely breathing could do to our boat with a nudge of its snout.

The whale goes under, the ocean smoothing over the spot of its shallow dive in what whalers called a fluke print. (They thought the calm water was caused by oil sloughing off the whale's skin.) The silence on deck is soon interrupted by cheers. As I relive the moment and imagine the future—"Did you hear it breathe?" "Do you think it'll breach?"—the whale resurfaces, now on our port. I lean over, holding tight to a shroud. The whale inhales and, leading with its right side, rolls under our ship. It reappears on our starboard, and I swing around the mast, grab another shroud, and lean over the boat's edge to catch a view. On this third resurfacing, the whale lingers, but soon I see more and more of its arched back, and then its tail, rise above the water, and the whale disappears.

What I remember most about this encounter is that I never saw the whole whale. The gray was longer than our catamaran, and as it surfaced—rostrum rising above the sea first, then blowhole, then the dorsal ridge's knobby knuckles, and finally its flukes—I saw only glimpses at a time. Never its flippers, never its belly. Never the entire whale. The sea hides much, if not all, of the animal.

Years later my wife teases me, upon our return from Hawai'i, about the hundreds of photos I've taken of water. "Look," I say to her, pointing at a black speck in the picture, "there's a whale." It's counterintuitive an animal so large is so hard to photograph. These animals, despite their size, move quickly. They surface, though I don't know where that will be, and by the time I have my camera up, they dive, their fifty-ton bodies again vanished.

My family, friends, and colleagues know I chase whales, and so they send notice whenever whales are in the news. Last year, from four people, I was told about the release of Nick Pyenson's *Spying on Whales*. Pyenson is a whale paleontologist at the Smithsonian, and he speaks to how hard it is to see and study these animals. The difficulty comes from a simple fact: whales live in a part of the world inaccessible to us. Pyenson explains:

> Blue whales, fin whales, right whales, and bowhead whales . . . are the largest animals, by weight, ever to have evolved. They just don't happen to live close to anywhere where most people would see them. Even the largest animals of all time are still elusive and rarely seen on an instrumented planet with several billion people.

Our instrumented, surveilled society can take and post photos of peregrine falcons in their nests atop skyscrapers, of celebrities on their vacation yachts, of back-alley drug deals. We have no problem acquiring footage of any number of furtive activities, but the whale remains out of view. Only recently have humans even had the means to see the whale within its own watery world. In another book given me, historian Philip Hoare writes,

> It was only after we had seen the Earth from orbiting spaceships that the first free-swimming whale was photographed underwater. The first underwater footage of sperm whales, off the coast of Sri Lanka, was not taken until 1984; our images of these huge placid creatures moving gracefully and silently through the ocean are more recent than the use of personal computers. We knew what the world looked like before we knew what the whale looked like.

The same year sperm whales were first filmed under water, Smithsonian published *The World's Whales: The Complete Illustrated Guide*. (This, too, was a gift; a friend found it in a used bookstore and mailed it across the country to me, along with four other whale books.) I cannot help but read the title as ironic: this "complete illustrated guide" is far from complete, relying on sketches of whales—such as the pygmy sperm whale, southern bottlenose whale, Longman's and Hector's and Hubbs' beaked whales—when photographs are not available.

I am sympathetic to the book and its project. Hoare reminds me that "even now there are beaked whales or ziphiids, known only from bones washed up on remote beaches—esoteric, deep-sea animals with strange markings which biologists have never seen alive or dead, so little studied that their status is 'data deficient.'" There's a lot of deficient data when studying whales, and so there are a lot of drawings in *The World's Whales*, an artist's best approximation of what these leviathans look like.

Decades after the book's publication, we still do not know all that swims within the sea. Even when I may have a sense of what I'm looking at through my binoculars, it's hard to make definitive claims about a whale sighting. That gray I saw in Santa Barbara— the one that came right alongside our boat—I don't know whether it was female or male, or how old it was, or what it might have weighed. I know it was a gray whale longer than our catamaran, and that's it.

Consider, too, what little is known about how a whale's body works. Pyenson notes, "No one has ever recorded the beating heart of a wild baleen whale. We don't know how fast or slow the heart of a rorqual whale, such as the blue whale, races when diving, feeding, or even sleeping." Pyenson says this in a book published in 2018; in 2019, a little progress was made. Using electrodes suctioned onto the whale's back, a Stanford biologist monitored a diving blue whale's pulse. Its heart rate dips as low as two beats a minute.

Such research is difficult (in most cases, impossible) because, again, the world whales inhabit is inaccessible to humans, but also (and more so) because "the parameters of their daily lives defy many of our tools to measure them: they travel over spans of whole oceans, dive to depths where light does not reach, and live for human life-times—and even longer." The difference between this life and mine is comical: orcas eat upward of three hundred pounds of salmon a day; I'll finish half a trout at dinner. A newborn blue whale is twenty-three feet long; my son was twenty-two inches. When migrating, gray whales swim seventy-five miles a day; I walk four, maybe five.

I can show my students underwater photos of whales, videos too, pictures of carcasses washed ashore, but still the class will have questions that should be easy to answer yet are not—like what color a whale is. "Underwater, [sperm whales] appear ghostly grey filtered through the ocean's blue," Hoare writes, "but in sunlight they appear brown or even sleekly black, depending on their age and sex. They may even verge on a dandified purple or lavender, with pale freckles scattered on their underbellies." Gray, brown, black, purple, laven-der, polka-dotted—I'm unable to determine something as seemingly simple as the color of a whale.

We don't even know how many kinds of whales there are. The best whale researchers are at a loss. This gives Hoare a bit of humility and wonder: "New cetaceans are still being identified in the twenty-first century, and we would do well to remember that the world harbours animals bigger than ourselves, which we have yet to see; that not everything is catalogued and claimed and digitized."

Herman Melville had a sense about this. In an 1851 letter he writes, "Leviathan is not the biggest fish;—I have heard of Krakens." I think of the Cadborosaurus supposedly swimming off Washington's coast, or the many, many sea monsters populating sea shanties and sailors' stories, or the narluga—a little-seen hybrid of the narwhal and beluga. In 2010, the rarest whale in the world and her calf washed ashore in New Zealand, so rare that the corpse was initially misidentified as a Gray's beaked whale. DNA testing later showed the animal to be something else: the spade-toothed beaked whale. Next to nothing is known of this whale; prior to these specimens, the sole artifacts scientists had were three partial skulls. In 2014, a new species of whale—the *karasu*, Japanese for raven—was discovered washed ashore in Alaska. In 2015, another new whale species, the Omura's whale, was confirmed. And in 2019, what could be a new species of killer whale was discovered in New Zealand.

The other day, I sent a postcard of a blue whale. The caption read: "THE LARGEST KNOWN ANIMAL ON EARTH." Might there be others, larger still?

"I was determined to know beans," confesses Henry David Thoreau. This is no small feat. Thoreau writes of sowing and harvesting beans at his cabin on Walden Pond, of cultivating them, of watching the birds above while he toils in the fields below, of the "intimate and curious acquaintance one makes with various kinds of weeds." He isn't in a hurry. "As I had little aid from horses or cattle, or hired men or boys, or improved implements of husbandry, I was much slower, and became much more intimate with my beans than usual." There is a sense, here, that if you want to know beans, to be "intimate with" them, to know them such that you can call them "*my* beans," you must have your hands in the soil, your fingernails and knees blackened, your shirt sodden, earth smeared across your brow. You must do the work yourself. You must take your time. You must work slowly, and this slow work becomes part of Thoreau's daily routine, tending his beans morning and night. "I came to love my rows, my beans," he writes. "I cherish them, I hoe them, early and late I have an eye on them; and this is my day's work."

I come to Thoreau after reading literary critic Richard Poirier in a graduate seminar in English, Poirier writing some 120 years after Thoreau and responding to him:

> How does anyone "know beans"? More perplexing still, how does anyone know that he knows them? . . . The answer is that you "know" a thing and know that you know it only when "work" begins to yield a language that puts you and something else, like a field, at a point of vibrant intersection.

Poirier claims the hoeing itself becomes a way of knowing, and this work begins to yield a language, this language making it possible to know something, which, for Thoreau, is beans. And you can know that you know something only once an engagement with the unknown creates "a language," Poirier's "a" here implying there are other languages, too, that might be a way of knowing, the language beginning to be yielded in this instance just one of many, many possibilities.

For Poirier, though, this language is fleeting. He says work "*begins to yield*" the words—not that it *yields*. The *beginning* suggests this knowing is nascent, inchoate. So too, Poirier says these words sit at a "point of vibrant intersection." They are alive, yes, but something cannot remain *vibrant* forever. These words are ephemeral, a language revealing itself momentarily only to then become elusive again as soon as it is found, as soon as it begins to yield itself—much like the whale.

So, Thoreau is determined to know beans. To know them, he must first hoe them, and from that work, learn how to talk about them, how to write about them, how to think about them, how to use language to make sense of, manipulate, and organize his world in relation to them—and this can happen only through the work itself, temporary as this knowing may be.

Ishmael is determined to know whales. Narrating his voyage aboard the *Pequod*, he sails under Captain Ahab, chasing an animal that spends a fraction of its life at the surface, an animal humans are seldom able to see. The crew does not see their first whale until chapter 47 of *Moby-Dick*, 171 pages into the novel. That whale escapes. And while Captain Ahab himself is shrouded in mystery (Ishmael doesn't see him until a quarter of the way through the book), Moby Dick more so. I read of him taking Ahab's leg; Ishmael and others in the novel tell me stories of Moby Dick's encounters with the *Jeroboam*, the *Town-Ho*, the *Samuel Enderby*, the *Rachel*, and the *Delight*; I read glimpses of what may (or may not) be Moby Dick in the mysterious spirit spout that appears at night, leading the *Pequod* onward; but I—alongside Ishmael, Ahab, and the rest of the crew—do not raise Moby Dick until chapter 133, a mere nineteen pages from the end of the 410-page book.

But Ishmael persists. He wants to know these animals, and so, drawing from Scoresby, Beale, Cuvier, Hunter, Lesson, Linnæus, Browne, Cheever, and others—Ishmael apparently reads widely—he lays out a taxonomy of the whale. Ishmael admits this is "no easy task. The classification of the constituents of a chaos, nothing less is here essayed." He then concedes "it is in vain to attempt a clear classification of the Leviathan," but he hopes "subsequent laborers" will continue the work he begins. And so he lists various species of whale: the *Sperm Whale*, the *Right Whale*, the *Fin Back Whale*, the *Humpbacked Whale*, the *Razor Back Whale*, the *Sulphur Bottom Whale*, the *Grampus*, the *Black Fish*, the *Narwhale*, the *Killer*, the *Thrasher*, the *Huzza Porpoise*, the *Algerine Porpoise*, and the *Mealy-mouthed Porpoise*.

It's curious that Ishmael refers to each whale as a "chapter," and he groups the above whale chapters into three larger categories, also using book language: "I. The FOLIO WHALE; II. The OCTAVO WHALE; III. The DUODECIMO WHALE." Dan Beachy-Quick suggests these divisions are more than "pleasurable wit." They are, in fact, "a claim," and the claim is this: "A whale is a book, and a book is a whale." If that is true, then "Ishmael's writing of *Moby-Dick* . . . is itself an act of whaling." By opening the book, then, I open the whale, participating in its flensing.

After giving this catalogue—or, should I say, writing this book—Ishmael calls it into question, noting that "there are a rabble of uncertain, fugitive, half-fabulous whales, which, as an American whale-man, I know by reputation, but not personally." True to his exhaustive character, he lists them too, though not italicizing the names as he did before, the difference in font suggesting, perhaps, a difference in certainty: "The Bottle-Nose Whale; the Junk Whale; the Pudding-Headed Whale; the Cape Whale; the Leading Whale; the Cannon Whale; the Scragg Whale; the Coppered Whale; the Elephant Whale; the Iceberg Whale; the Quog Whale; the Blue Whale; &c." His "&c" recalls the postcard I sent, both signaling this inventory is not (nor ever could be) complete. Ishmael knows this. "I now leave my cetological System standing thus unfinished. . . . This whole book is but a draught—nay, but the draught of a draught. Oh, Time, Strength, Cash, and Patience!" Ishmael's cetology is abridged—necessarily, unavoidably, and regrettably so.

Even though he cannot catalogue all whales, later Ishmael attempts to correct what the public thinks they look like. He devotes three chapters to monstrous pictures of whales—"I shall ere long paint to you as well as one can without canvas, something like the true form of the whale as he actually appears"—and just as he finishes his cetology with a note of defeat, he realizes, too, that creating an accurate picture of the whale is a fool's errand. Trying to understand what the whale looks like based on those washed ashore doesn't work, he says: that is like trying to know what a ship looks like based on a shipwreck. So too, the skeleton isn't useful, since a skeleton doesn't look much like the animal it's inside.

Ishmael sees no way around these obstacles, and he concludes, "the great Leviathan is that one creature in the world which must remain unpainted to the last." Some paintings may be more accurate than others, he admits, but in the end "there is no earthly way of finding out precisely what the whale really looks like." The only option, he says, is going on a whaleship, but that is just too dangerous: "You run no small risk of being eternally stove and sunk by him."

Today, though, I don't have to go on a whaleship to see a whale. We're no longer in the nineteenth century. I have means of approaching the whale, of getting close, of documenting it, of researching its behaviors, of charting its migrations and feeding grounds, of photographing it and filming it—and yet, while I want to push against Ishmael, I cannot ignore his concluding words, words of caution, words with an ominous tone: "Wherefore it seems to me you had best not be too fastidious in your curiosity touching this Leviathan."

Because I am a writing teacher, I read books on pedagogy, and Stacey Waite has written the best one I've read in a long time, *Teaching Queer: Radical Possibilities for Writing and Knowing*. Waite faces a problem common to all teachers of writing: her students often want to write essays on controversial topics, essays that parrot what the student already believes, or champion commonplaces, rather than inquiring into the issue. To resist this impulse, Waite "invite[s] students to write about these subjects in ways that might illuminate the limits of their own experience and knowledge, in ways that might reveal their own failure to know." She does this because she's concerned with "the already failing extent of our various knowledges." It is there, where knowledge fails, that possibility resides.

Pushing students out of their comfort in what they know—rather, what they think they know that they know—Waite gives them this (very hard) assignment:

> Before you begin this project, you should compose two lists that form a kind of lyrical essay. There should be 20–25 sentences on each list. The first list will be 20–25 sentences that start with the words, "I do not know." And the second list will be sentences that start with the words, "I cannot know." This assignment calls you to begin with what you do not and cannot know about this subject. It asks you to begin by recording the limits of your own knowledge and experience. It asks you to take seriously the idea that you don't already know, in a full way, your position on this subject, even if you feel that you do. It asks you to acknowledge that all knowledge is partial knowledge, and to begin your

project with a full examination of what you have failed to know, uncover, or see about this project. If you want to write about this subject, you must consider how to make your essay or project reflect both what you think you know and what you do not, or cannot, know.

For Waite's students, this assignment produces unease, an awareness that knowledge is fluid, contextual, limited, contingent. It also produces a space of possibility, of wonder, a willingness to venture into, rather than turn from, the unknown.

Consider this, something (as Waite says) we do not, and cannot, know: "Orcas may not be very intelligent humans," neuroscientist Lori Marino says, "but humans are really stupid orcas." The reason is that not only does the orca brain have more wrinkling than any other animal on the planet—this is called gyrification, and it "increase[s] the amount of total cortical nerve tissue dedicated to processing information"—but also "orca brains have something that humans and land animals don't, a highly developed set of brain lobes called the paralimbic system." Marino explains:

> We don't know what it does. We can only infer. But what we do know is that this is an area that is not identifiably elaborated at all in humans and many other mammals. So, there's something about those cetacean brains that required them to develop something, probably having to do with processing emotions in some other way, that caused this lobe to elaborate. We don't know.
>
> It is a very mysterious part, probably the most compelling part of the brain of orcas and dolphins. Because again, we're not used to other animals having things we don't have, in our brain.

Commenting on Marino's research, journalist David Neiwert writes that this paralimbic system "may enable some brain function we can't envision because we lack it." The orca thinks thoughts we are unable to think, let alone even begin to conceive. *We can't envision because we lack it.* And if I were to push into this unknown, I suspect I'd find within it further mystery—mystery I wouldn't be able to articulate. *We can't envision because we lack it.* My brain is simply unable. *We can't envision because we lack it.* I do not know. I cannot know.

There is a moment in the mass, before the breaking of the bread, when the priest says, "Let us proclaim the mystery of the faith," and the people respond, "Christ has died; Christ is risen; Christ will come again." How is this not audacious, to *proclaim*—which suggests certainty, confidence, assuredness—a *mystery*—which suggests uncertainty, doubt, wandering? This tension is central to a faith that asks for belief in things unbelievable, a faith that asks for a proclamation of, and peace with, not knowing.

Thinking he'd beached his boat on an island, Saint Brendan of Clonfert celebrated the Eucharist on the back of a whale.

Still, Ishmael is determined to know whales. He offers measurements: "a Sperm Whale of the largest in magnitude, between eighty-five and ninety feet in length, and something less than forty feet in its fullest circumference, such a whale will weigh at least ninety tons." Technically, he's right. This whale would weigh *at least* ninety tons. But Ishmael has grossly underestimated the weight of such a whale. Even though he's in the realm of myth with his ninety-foot sperm whale, if such a whale were to exist, it would weigh upward of 274 tons.

I come to that figure using the WhaleScale, an app developed by North Carolina State University's Center for Marine Sciences and Technology "to inform decision-making during management of stranding events." Plug the length and species of a whale into the app and it gives the weight. This information could be useful when determining what size backhoe is needed to move a dead whale, or whether moving it is even possible.

A research librarian at my university pulls one of the many articles WhaleScale bases its figures on. I find in it a graph—familiar enough with its X and Y axes—with nine lines curving upward exponentially, one for each of the nine whales in the study. I run my finger along the dashed line for the sperm whale, its length topping out around nineteen meters, its weight around seventy tons. Ishmael's ninety-foot sperm whale is literally off the chart.

But how does someone even weigh a whale? There is no scale aboard the *Pequod* (let alone most modern ships) large enough to conduct such research. If one is to be weighed on land, it has to be cut up to fit most scales, losing flesh and bodily fluids. (The research informing WhaleScale takes lost blood and bodily fluids into account: 6 percent on baleen whales, 10 percent on sperm whales.) It could be hoisted from the water with a ship crane, many of which have scales, but those scales are often calibrated to tick off weight every thousand pounds; they're not precise. Compromises abound. It is difficult to determine a whale's color. It's harder to weigh it.

Length, though, is easier. In a group of islands northeast of Australia, on leave from another ship, Ishmael comes across a sperm whale skeleton. He measures it. The skeleton comes to seventy-two feet, its skull and jaw twenty, its backbone fifty. And again, Ishmael falls short of knowing: "The skeleton of the whale is by no means the mould of its invested form." The longest ribs are eight feet, Ishmael tells me, but the whale—fully fleshed and alive—would be at least sixteen feet tall at that point, "So that this rib only conveyed half of the true notion of the living magnitude of that part." He continues:

> How vain and foolish, then, thought I, for timid untraveled man to try to comprehend aright this wonderous whale, by merely poring over his dead attenuated skeleton. . . . No. Only in the heart of quickest perils; only when within the eddyings of his angry flukes; only on the profound unbounded sea, can the fully invested whale be truly and livingly found out.

Ishmael longs to know the whale, yet he realizes that measurement alone cannot fully account for the complexities, the nuances, and the dynamism of the leviathan—even as he is doing the very work Thoreau and Poirier say is necessary to know beans. He's at the point of vibrant intersection. His hands are inside the leviathan, he is tilling the soil, yet he laments, "Dissect him how I may, then, I but go skin deep; I know him not, and never will."

In the Book of Job, the Lord asks him a series of questions, beginning with this:

> "Where were you when I laid the foundation of the earth?
> Tell me, if you have understanding."

Demarcating the divine from Job's humanity, placing boundaries on Job's knowledge, on Job's ability to know, the questions continue:

> "Or who shut in the sea with doors
> when it burst out from the womb,
> when I made clouds its garment
> and thick darkness its swaddling band,
> and prescribed limits for it
> and set bars and doors,
> and said, 'Thus far shall you come, and no farther,
> and here shall your proud waves be stayed'?"

To this, Job has no response:

> "Behold, I am of small account; what shall I answer you?
> I lay my hand on my mouth."

But the questions keep coming, the Lord now turning to the whale.

> "Can you draw out Leviathan with a fishhook,
> or press down his tongue with a cord?"

Job stands there, silenced. It is a response not unlike Ishmael's when confronting the whale. "To grope down into the bottom of the sea after them; to have one's hands among the unspeakable foundations, ribs, and very pelvis of the world; this is a fearful thing," Ishmael confesses. "What am I that I should essay to hook the nose of this leviathan! The awful tauntings in Job might well appal me."

The Lord's tauntings appall Ishmael, and Job cannot respond to the Lord's questions. But we, today, do draw out Leviathan with a fishhook. We've been doing it for centuries.

"Can you put a rope in his nose
Or pierce his jaw with a hook?"

Yes.

"Will he make many pleas to you?
Will he speak to you soft words?"

Biologists are working to decode whale song.

"Will he make a covenant with you
To take him for your servant forever?"

So-called Whale Cowboys began capturing orcas in the 1960s.

"Will you play with him as with a bird,
Or will you put him on a leash for your girls?"

In marine parks, trainers ride whales, teach them to do cartwheels, and parade them before crowds.

"Will traders bargain over him?
Will they divide him up among the merchants?"

In Japan, you can buy whale steaks and whale bacon. In Norway, whale protein powder and whale vitamins.

"Can you fill his skin with harpoons?"

Yes.

"Or his head with fishing spears?"

Yes.

The Lord then warns Job with language that, for me, calls to mind the many accounts I've read of sperm whales fighting back against their whalers, the whales ramming hulls, their flukes crushing ships. Whalers referred to those flukes as "The Hand of God."

"Lay your hands on [the Leviathan];
Remember the battle—you will not do it again!
Behold, the hope of a man is false;
He is laid low even at the sight of him.
No one is so fierce that he dares to stir him up.
Who then is he who can stand before me?"

Millennia after this poetry was written, whalers are no longer laid low at the sight of a spout. Sitting in a rowboat, looking down on a whale harpooned and writhing in the depths below, Ishmael laments, "Is this the creature of whom it was once so triumphantly said—'Canst thou fill his skin with barbed irons? or his head with fish-spears?'" Ishmael dares stir up the Leviathan, he dares stand before him. And he will come to regret it.

Thoreau asks, "What shall I know of beans and beans of me?" In a sense, the whale already knows me for it knows humans. It knows the humans who hunt it, the humans who capture it, the humans whose ships strike it, the humans whose noise pollution impede its ability to hunt and navigate and communicate. And it knows, too, the humans who research it, who try to save it. By being human, I am complicit in all these acts; the whale knows me.

But what shall I know of whales? I grew up landlocked in eastern Washington, didn't see a whale until I was twenty-two, have never touched a live whale, have never swam with one, have never talked with one, haven't put in the biologist's hours upon hours upon hours of fieldwork.

I do, though, remember my first encounter with whales. I was seven, maybe eight, and my parents took me to a traveling exhibit. It was in a warehouse on the edge of town, near a now-defunct zoo. Together we walked into the darkened room. It was vast. Humid, too. And above us were whales. Life-size replicas made of molded plastic. An orca and a humpback, a gray, the centerpiece of the exhibit a blue whale. Whale song played overhead. The walls were painted to look like a kelp forest. Hanging from the ceiling, twisted strands of thin translucent green plastic. I pushed aside the seaweed as I made my way through the room. Below each whale were displays: *What do whales eat? Where do whales live?* I remember the whales only. I walked under them, terrified. The exhibit was not designed to be scary. It was supposed to be educational. But when I look back at it now, what I most remember is fear. Fear of looming, immobile leviathans, fear of their size, fear of the darkness, fear of the sea.

In her memoir *H Is for Hawk*, Helen Macdonald tells a similar story. When she was a young girl, her parents took her to a field to watch falconers. She'd begged to go, and she observes in silence the birds above and the men below. *"I'll remember this day forever,"* she tells herself, *"One day this will be me."* It's a defining moment in her life.

I did not know, standing among those whales, that one day I would so too be obsessed, but the warehouse awakened a curiosity. Later that summer, when my family sailed on Lake Pend Oreille, and my dad told of the fifty-foot sturgeon there (fishermen claimed to see her occasionally), I thought of that exhibit, thought of the creatures of the deep. I swam with an unease for what I shared the water with, or, rather, whose water I swam in. When I would see a suckerfish through my goggles—no matter how large—I would thrash toward our boat's ladder, hoist myself up, and wait until I was sure the fish had swum away before returning to the water, wanting, despite my fear, to be there, nonetheless.

After I left the whale hall, I began reading everything I could on whales (just as Macdonald, as a child, read everything she could on hawks), amassing a carefully curated library of whale books, beginning with Erich Hoyt's *Orca: The Whale Called Killer*. Hoyt's book is not at all one most elementary-aged children would read. Pages packed with small font, it's a scientific treatise coupled with first-person narrative, one of the earliest accounts from a researcher studying these animals. It has pictures, yes, but fewer of those than paragraph after paragraph after paragraph of a biologist's meticulous work. It's a far cry from *The Boxcar Children*.

Reading Hoyt, I began to understand the world through whales. My school bus became a humpback whale, my parents' Oldsmobile

Custom Cruiser station wagon a pilot whale. When I learned a human's digestive tract can reach thirty feet, I'd think "I've got a killer whale inside me." A road sign announcing a juncture in eight hundred feet translated to me as eight blue whales away.

Hoyt became my childhood companion, and I held him tight for years, his book more and more legible with each rereading. I'd soon have other bookish companions: Philip Hoare, Kathleen Jamie, Stacey Waite, Dan Beachy-Quick, David Bartholomae, the prophet Jonah. I reread them often. I load my messenger bag with them when I head to the coast in search of whales. I spend time inside their sentences, copying them by hand into my commonplace book, coming to understand my own work through its relationship to theirs.

And now, years later, I too am determined to know whales. I look at photographs taken with long lens and underwater cameras, at footage from helicopters and boats and skiffs and drones. I listen to live-streamed hydrophones, hoping to hear something, anything. I read reports from researchers trailing whales, scooping up their feces and using the DNA in that waste to chart family trees. I read necropsies of whales washed ashore. I read accounts on social media of viewing whales from boats, bridges, and beaches.

But my efforts alone are not enough. Nick Pyenson reminds me that answering big questions "requires pulling data and insights from multiple scientific disciplines, which is another way of saying that we need the perspectives of different kinds of science—and scientists—to untangle the monstrous challenges of the nearly inaccessible lives of whales." This is true. To know whales, biologists work alongside chemists alongside paleontologists alongside ecologists alongside physicists. I am none of these things. I am a writer, a teacher, and, perhaps, a cetologist. Even still, I want to work alongside these scientists, remembering that knowing, according to Poirier, happens only once work begins to yield a language. For me, that work is looking and finding through reading and writing, and the language it yields is different from the language of science. I hope to find a point of vibrant intersection where I might know beans. And know, too, that I cannot.

TWO } From a Distance

A window opening on nothing but the blank sky was endlessly
attractive to me; if I watched long enough, a bird or a cloud would
appear within the frame, and I watched with patience.

—Jayber,
in Wendell Berry's *Jayber Crow*

I spend a lot of time on beaches, binoculars raised, seeing nothing. I
should clarify: seeing not what I am there to see. I see tern, gull, seal,
sea lion, hawk, porpoise, salmon, crab, barnacle, sand dollar, starfish,
sea anemone, sea urchin, heron, eagle, egret, crow, dog, person—any
number of animals other than the whale. My son has a book that offers some guidance: "If you want to see a whale," it tells me, "you will
need time for waiting and time for looking and time for wondering 'is
that a whale?' and time for realizing, 'no, it's just a bird.'"

Seems unlikely to mistake bird for whale, but I do. A disturbance on
the water, a splash mistaken for a fin, a bobbing hunk of wood, a crab
pot, a buoy—ever hopeful, often disappointed. The book continues:
"If you want to see a whale you will need a not-so-comfy chair and a
not-too-cozy blanket because sleeping eyes can't watch for whales and
whales won't wait for watching." You can't be watching the roses, or
the boats, or the pelicans, or the inchworms, or the clouds either. "If
you want to see a whale," the book says in its final pages, "keep both
eyes on the sea and wait . . . and wait . . . and wait . . ." The ellipses here
are in the original, this last sentence spread over six pages, its punctu-
ation a lesson in waiting.

So I wait, and wait, and wait, eyes on the water, and I find a kinship
there. I think of fellow watcher and waiter Kathleen Jamie and her

books *Sightlines* and *Findings*, collections of essays on Scotland and the remote islands surrounding it. Jamie often comes with me to the shore. I read her prose there, think of my own, and wait. I was introduced to her work by one of my teachers, partly for the beauty of her sentences but more so because she often finds herself among whales.

Jamie's on a bluff, watching a gannet colony, when she sees—or, thinks she sees—something in the water. "It was as though someone had leaned over my shoulder and drawn, among the resting birds, a quick vertical line with a pencil. That's all. A quick line." She tries to discern what the fleeting line might have been. A mirage? A creel marker? Jamie's first inclination is to dismiss what she saw, but she knows better. "It was probably nothing, so I said nothing, but kept looking. That's what the keen-eyed naturalists say. Keep looking. Keep looking, even when there's nothing much to see."

Though *If You Want to See a Whale* is but a children's book, and I have no idea whether Jamie's read it (I doubt so), I read her watching as it advises. I try to as well. Keep both eyes on the water. Ignore all distractions. Flowers, birds, and boats are not whales, and I am at the beach to watch not for these things but whales.

Yet, to some extent, I must pay attention to each and every distraction. I must watch the birds and the boats and the crab pots, the deadheads and the knots of kelp floating by, the bait balls that attract gulls and (sometimes) seals, which (sometimes) then attract whales. I must, because, as Jamie says, "That way your eye learns what's common, so when the uncommon appears, your eye will tell you." Just as Jamie does, I must attune my eye, my brain, my self to the ordinary. The thin pencil line she saw, thought of ignoring, but then kept looking for, knowing it was not ordinary, soon resurfaced, gannets scattering as an orca's six-foot dorsal fin cut the water.

On a recent trip to the beach, I bought a field guide to sea birds. I see them much more than I see whales. I plan to learn their names.

Ishmael acknowledges that "it might seem an absurdly hopeless task thus to seek out one solitary creature in the unhooped oceans of this planet." A curious word, *unhooped*. It means "unbound," and given that sperm whales do not follow migration routes, tracking them is, indeed, absurd, especially tracking a single whale. But Captain Ahab tries. In his cabin, he has "a large wrinkled roll of yellowish sea charts." Next to him, old ship logs piled high. Using these, along with reports of whale sightings, he maps sperm whale feeding grounds against the prevailing currents and charts a course for the *Pequod*.

I, too, keep a chart. It's number 18421, published by the US Department of Commerce and the National Oceanic and Atmospheric Administration, and it covers from the Strait of Juan de Fuca in the south to the Strait of Georgia in the north. On the east is Bellingham Bay and to the west is Victoria, British Columbia. In the map's center are the San Juan Islands. There are no bridges to these islands. You need your own boat to get to most, but the big four (San Juan, Lopez, Shaw, and Orcas) are accessible via ferry. My chart has the ferry routes and the shipping lanes. I once heard that to become a ferry captain in Washington, applicants must draw, from memory, a complete map of the area, including the depths of all the channels, just in case their GPS should fail. I do not know how accurate this map from memory needs to be. There are more than four hundred islands in the Salish Sea.

I have turned my chart into a log, of sorts, marking the location of every whale I've seen: 11 June 2006, five orcas from the J-pod near Canadian waters at Point Roberts; 19 August 2008, thirteen transient orcas off Saturna Island; 6 July 2012, two from J-pod, joined by a whale from L-pod, swimming up San Juan Island's western side; 20 September 2016, a gray whale in Friday Harbor. On the map's margins I list whales I've seen outside the bounds of the page: gray whales in Santa Barbara; a minke in Maine; gray whales and humpbacks and minkes elsewhere in Washington; humpbacks in Hawaiʻi; an orca at the Discovery Park lighthouse.

My chart pales next to the one kept online by the Orca Network, which collects all reported whale sightings in the area, including some reaching down to California and up to British Columbia. It's covered with icons placed where orcas, grays, humpbacks, minkes, fins, dolphins, and pseudorcas have been seen. Each week, Orca

Network posts the unedited sighting reports they've received. These reports come both from researchers and from regular people out on beaches or in their boats, on docks or bridges or ferries or hillsides.

Below is the full report for 14 May 2018. It's long, I know, but I present the whole thing for a sense of how a day unfolds. Some entries mention photographs, which I've not included. I've reorganized the report chronologically, but the italics, bold font, repeated words, typos, and misspellings are unedited. They're part of the story, how it's recorded and then told, this one beginning in a bedroom where a woman is awakened by a whale:

> Early this morning, I woke at **2:00 am the the sound of gray whale blows**. The water was totally calm, no wind, all quite. I meandered back into my dreams listening to the whale go farther and farther away into the night. North from Pebble Beach. —Peg Boley

> WA State Ferries called in a report of **two grays seen from the Mukilteo Clinton ferry headed NW at 7:40 am** (the message said southbound, headed NW, but we think they may have meant the whales were south of the ferry run, headed NW?)

> Coastal killer whales—May 14—Received a call from Robert, at the Winchester Bay RV park in OR, near the marina where the **Umpqua River** comes out, he reported **a male orca with a 6' dorsal fin in the marina this morning**, then swimming upriver quite a ways, then passing close by the marina and RV Park again on his way back out to sea. They were very surprised to see him!

> Gray whales (South Puget Sound)—May 14—**Budd Inlet**—Update from CRC with link: **A gray whale** was spotted this morning near Olympia, WA. We have been tracking the movements of several gray whales sighted in southern Puget Sound in recent weeks. Thus far there have been indications that this year may be one of elevated gray whale mortality, with potentially more whales in poor body condition. Read more about these indications on our website. —Cascadia Research Collective

> **10:50 a.m.**—**Gray** is still in **Budd Inlet** very close to the Port of Olympia. That is WAY toward the southern most point of Puget Sound. —Kim Merriman

10:50 a.m—**Gray whale near northwest tip Hat Island,** seen from Sandy Point, Whidbey. Nice backlit blows visible with no magnification needed. —Steve Smith

Minke whales—May 14—There was a group of **six minkes feeding in north Admiralty at about 11am**. I think just **north of point Wilson midchannel**. Will send photos later. —Ariel Yseth

Whale blow and a sailboat . . . Posted **11:00 a.m**—Maybe the **same two** we were watching in the Saratoga Passage until a few minutes ago, headed north, just south of Bells Beach about an hour ago. —Photo by Kathy Bridges, May 14, 2018

11:08 a.m—Single whale spotted from **Point Wilson** in Fort Worden. Likely **minke** or possibly a single orca. Headed south, mid Channel. Only saw one time and couldn't get a picture! —Allison Stewart Bishins

11:13 a.m—This is probably whale Steve Smith noted . . . whale mid channel **between Gedney and Tulalip,** traveling south with occasional deep dives. —Lori Christopher

Bigg's killer whales—**12:05 p.m**—T101s **mid Haro** going north aiming for Lime Kiln right now! —Monika Wieland, OBI

With reports of whales, we set off towards Sidney Island in Canadian waters! Passing Colville Island by Lopez Is, we checked on the harbor seals hauled out, then saw Dall's porpoise along San Juan Island, continuing north to find the T101s and T102 again! So cool to see these 4 whales two days in a row! We had great views of them as they passed **Sidney Island,** still northbound. Homeward bound we checked on the seals and Steller sea lions on Spieden Island. It was another spectacularly sunny day and our trip home inter islands added to the amazing day! **T101A (born 1993) and T101B (born 1997) on the left, Mom T101 (born 1973) in the middle, and T102 (born 1984) on the right.** —Jill Hein, volunteer naturalist, Mystic Sea

Saw this beauty coming out of **Olympia Harbor about 1:45pm** today . . . surfaced a few times and then went deep, but appeared to be heading north. We went in the west side of the port at **1:45** and it was coming out from near the log facility headed north. When we left at **3:30 p.m.** it was still in the open area just outside the entrances to the ports. —Cari Black

Dall's porpoise—May 14 . . . Passing Colville Island by Lopez Is, we checked on the harbor seals hauled out, then saw **Dall's porpoise along San Juan Island** . . . There were **10–12 in the group**. Fast! —Photo by Jill Hein, Mystic Sea, May 14, 2018

At **2:40 p.m.** this afternoon, we saw **a gray traveling south off of Pebble Beach**, Camano. —Peg Boley

3:31 p.m.—Single grey whale in Langley at the whale bell location! Close to shore! —Marcie Barney Goldberg

5:02 p.m.—Still feeding north of the beach walk. May be heading back south! —Connie Bickerton

5:12 p.m.—gray staying in the same area, not traveling much.

5:30 p.m—Heard the **gray whale** exhaltion and then saw her/him surface . . . looks like heading northbound right now. —Gayle Swigart

(*Photos to supplement Gayle's report which was included in our Whale Sighting Report date May 15). Lovely illuminated exhalation of this beautiful gray whale who has been in Puget Sound for several weeks. Here s/he is on the 2nd of two consecutive days spent in Budd Inlet; this day deep in the inlet off downtown Olympia waterfront.*) —Photo by Gayle Swigart, late/afternoon/early evening May 14, 2018

May 14—Possession Sound and South Saratoga Passage—Another gray traveling north at **Pebble Beach, Camano at 6:00 pm**. —Peg Boley

6:34 p.m.—Two grays actively feeding at the **seaplane base** (NAS Whidbey, Crescent Harbor). —Photo by Christine Sweger Miller, May 14, 2018

We also had a message tonight about a whale in Olympia, off **704 Columbia st**. by the Anthony's restaurant. Call was from WA State Patrol, at **6:54 pm**, relaying a report from someone, they thought it was a gray and that it might be lost.

May 14—North Saratoga Passage, Oak Harbor area—**7:06 p.m.—Gray at Crescent Harbor**, can't believe we are still getting visits! —Christine Hawkins

These reports are, at once, definitive (these people *did* see something) yet inconclusive (or, at least, they think they did) as suggested by phrases like "appeared to be heading north," "possibly a single orca," "looks like heading northbound," "maybe the same two we were watching in the Saratoga Passage." There's excitement (all those exclamation points!) coupled with uncertainty (Swigart doesn't know what pronoun to use when referring to the whale she saw). Six minkes are seen near Point Wilson around 11:00 a.m., and then, at 11:08, reported again, though this time the viewer, Allison Stewart Bishins, is unsure whether the lone whale she sees is a minke or an orca. Her confusion is understandable: minkes have a small dorsal fin not unlike that on a female orca or an orca calf. But I wonder what happened to the other five whales reported only eight minutes earlier, which makes me then wonder whether this single whale is a different whale altogether. Bishins saw something out there, but she and I don't—and never will—know what it was.

As I read this report, rich as it is, I sense it's woefully incomplete. Of course every whale could never be sighted, recorded, and archived. But watchers try. Peg Boley gives three reports on the day. Steve Smith sees a gray at 10:50, and twenty-three minutes later, Lori Christopher spots it again. Cascadia Research reports another gray spending its morning loitering in Budd Inlet, and later, Kim Merriman reports on it too. (I assume it's the same whale.) These efforts to record where whales go are important; incomplete as they are, they still provide data.

I am most drawn, however, to these reports as pieces of writing. They read as excerpts from a diary, intimate glimpses into how someone experiences joy ("Close to shore!," "Only saw one time and couldn't get a picture!," "can't believe we are still getting visits!") or concern ("it might be lost," "more whales in poor body condition"). Perhaps it's the need to get word out about what was seen that produces the many typos in the reports—repeated words, misspellings, unconventional capitalization—as well as the inconsistent formatting and inconsistencies in what data are collected. These could all be read as lazy but I read urgency. Content overpowers correctness.

I have sympathy for Ahab and his map, his methods. On 11 June 2006, I saw J2 and J8, and six years later, on 6 July, I saw both again. It's possible, and quite common, to run into the same whale multiple times. So, like Ahab, I scrutinize my map, the Orca Network's sighting archives, hydrophone recordings of whales in the area, and my own log of where and when I've seen which whales, and I plan accordingly: a weekend trip to the islands. My wife and son will be out of town. I'll take my dog, sleep in the back of the car, and search for whales.

Ahab was looking for a single whale that could be anywhere in the vast waters covering the earth. I'm looking for any species of whale in an area much, much smaller. Washington has 3,026 miles of shoreline. If I were standing on a beach looking over open ocean, the horizon would be three miles out, and I'd be able to see three miles up the coast and three miles down, a total area of roughly fourteen square miles. But here, in the Salish Sea, any view of open water is blocked by islands. The area I'm able to see from most beaches is five, perhaps six, square miles.

As I write this, in winter 2020, seventy-two resident killer whales live in these waters and another large group of transient orcas pass through often. Each year some twenty-seven thousand gray whales migrate along the coast from Alaska to Baja. Humpback, minke, and fin whales visit Washington as well. It would seem, then, that the odds of me seeing a whale—any whale—are much better than Ahab's finding Moby Dick. And yet, he found his whale, while I, sitting on the beach, trip after trip after trip to the water, hours spent binoculars to face, rarely see any.

Perhaps my problem is that I am on land and not in a boat. Once, in Hawai'i, I stood on the deck of a sailboat, yards from a humpback and her two-month-old calf, the calf staying close to her mother's side. I thought of my wife and our nursing son. The captain had turned off our engine but we were close. Too close. I could see the white of their pectoral fins under the water, could smell the whales. Could smell, too, the diesel from our ship. I regret this moment, this intrusion. Some of my closest encounters with whales have come at their expense. We "best not be too fastidious," Ishmael warns.

And so I will go to the beach, the choice of beach over boat likely stymying my chances of seeing a whale but choosing beach anyway. I want to honor the whale's prior claim to the ocean, honor its sovereignty, honor an animal within its own habitat, a habitat that—miles out to sea—does not (and perhaps should not) include humans.

Of her teaching, Stacey Waite says, "I try to be patient—I try to wait the way I wait for the train. Confident it will arrive. Not exactly sure of the precise moment, but soon." I want to be able to say the same about my waiting on the beach, that I wait with confidence, that I wait with assurance, with a hope for what will happen soon—but I have no such confidence. I wait for something that more often than not never arrives.

Most days, I wait at my computer. Orcasound maintains a network of hydrophones strategically placed throughout the Salish Sea. There's one between Snug Harbor and Andrews Bay, one beneath the main pier of the Seattle Aquarium, another under the pier of the Port Townsend Marine Science Center, another under the pellet plant pier at Neah Bay, and a final one at Lime Kiln State Park. Each hydrophone livestreams online, and Lime Kiln is my stream of choice. It's on San Juan Island's west side, near a quarry that began operations in 1860. A lighthouse was built in 1919. Below the lighthouse is a kelp forest, and the prevailing currents push salmon into the kelp, which then sometimes attracts orcas. My wife and I went there on our honeymoon, hoping to see whales. We saw nothing.

And most days, I hear nothing. But I listen anyway—to ship traffic, to the steady glug-glug-glug of water lapping against the hydrophone; it's a pleasant white noise, if nothing else—because, on rare occasion, the whales come. One afternoon, while meeting with two students in my office, the hydrophone streaming in the background, we heard them. A slurred trumpet call, almost, a melody I could never whistle, a sound my mouth could never produce. Our conversation halts. The students hadn't noticed the white noise but they are taken back at hearing whales. People who listen to the hydrophone regularly can distinguish one pod's calls from another. I am learning to listen.

And I am still learning to wait. I'm not very good at it. Kathleen Jamie likens this kind of waiting to faith: "Whale-watching, cetacean-watching proceeds like a kind of theology—by glimpses, sightings, a dorsal fin, a rolling back. A pursuit for the regretful; all might-have-beens and what-did-we-miss?" I notice her use of *pursuit* so close to *theology*. I read it alongside an essay by Isaac Anderson, who calls the Psalms a "literature of pursuit." I don't think he's read Jamie, but I read him with her in mind: the Psalms "were texts born of the belief that God responds to language, can be flushed out into the open, by those humble enough, or perhaps lonely enough, to pray." Anderson himself prays the Psalms because he believes "God is not extinct, but only hidden. Concealed in the blur of daily life. Camouflaged, always, but on rare occasions identifiable."

It's as if Anderson is writing about whales—hidden, concealed, camouflaged, on rare occasions identifiable—but this passage comes in an essay about bird-watching, and later he writes of efforts to document the Lord God bird, a rare (perhaps extinct) woodpecker that may (or may not) have been videotaped in 2004 by bird-watcher Geoff Hill:

> Even with a camera at his side, he couldn't get a shot. Likewise for the handful of his colleagues who have claimed similar sightings—fourteen in all. Notebooks swell with their efforts to apprehend what they've seen. Their records, like many of the Psalms, are a literature of pursuit.

The birdwatcher's fieldnotes chronicle a chase across the years. It's a catalogue of nothingness—except the rare moment when the bird is seen.

Last year, a copy of Victor Scheffer's *The Year of the Whale* appeared in my university mailbox. I am often gifted whale memorabilia. Figurines, rocks and seashells and tree nuts that look like cetaceans, a bottle of Southern Right wine, toys, baby bibs, T-shirts, most of it accompanied with a note. A friend gave me a sailor's knife, its bone hilt inscribed with a line from the hymn sung in Father Mapple's church: "No more the whale did me confine." I do not know where Scheffer came from though. There was no note and no name on his inside cover. The marginalia inside offers no clues either.

Though Melville reminds us the whale lives an "unwritten life," Scheffer tries to give an account of a sperm whale calf's first year. *The Year of the Whale* is fiction grounded in cetology. These animals spend the majority of their lives hidden from view. Given how little time they are at the surface, it is "more apt to call the sperm whale a surfacer rather than a diver." But for all this mystery, Scheffer makes a surprising claim: "If, by some magic of electronics, man could spy on the intimate life of a whale, even for a week, he would turn away, bored and restless."

Would I? Turn away out of boredom, the curtain pulled back and the mystery now mundane? (Ishmael does admit that "in a whaler wonders soon wane.") Or might I turn away for another reason?

Consider this, from Annie Dillard. She tells of traveling across the state, through a tunnel carved through an avalanche in the Cascades, to a central Washington hotel, rising at 6:00 a.m. to drive outside Yakima, then trekking up a five-hundred-foot hill, wading through hordes of like-minded people, all in hopes of witnessing an eclipse.

She and her husband wait. The sun rises and they wait. They watch their shadows and they wait—wait as they might wait for the train, confident it will arrive (Dillard knows what time the eclipse should happen) though not sure it will (she doubts the weather will cooperate). But arrive it does. The moon passes between earth and sun. The light changes. Everything takes on a metallic hue. "The world was wrong," Dillard writes. Darkness comes. People begin screaming. And then, "an odd thing happened." As soon as totality ends and the sun peeks out from behind the moon, "We all hurried away. We were born and bored at a stroke. We rushed down the hill. We found our car; we saw other people streaming down the hillsides; we joined the highway traffic and drove away. We never looked back."

Both Dillard and Scheffer use *bored* to describe people turning away. But as Dillard uses it, *bored* isn't just boredom. It's fatigue from being face-to-face with the ineffable. "But enough is enough," she writes. "One turns at last even from glory itself with a sigh of relief." You can only sustain it so long. (This is why Catholics kneel before the host.) Dillard continues: "From the depths of mystery, and even from the heights of splendor, we bounce back and hurry for the latitudes of home." She and her hillside companions recoil from the extra-ordinary, turning back toward the comfort of the ordinary, the everyday, the familiar. They just can't take any more.

Dillard notes that people screamed during the eclipse. Writing teachers have a term for that: the interjection, an utterance when no other will do, an utterance when syntax is unable to carry a thought. I think, again, of Jamie:

> The reason I'd come to the end of the road to walk along the cliffs is because language fails me there. If we work always in words, sometimes we need to recuperate in a place where language doesn't join up, where we're thrown back on a few elementary nouns. Sea. Bird. Sky.

Jamie intentionally places herself in a position for language to fail her. She relies on the failure. It rejuvenates her. She grasps for a few nouns and holds them close. The nouns become *elementary*—not in the sense of grammar school but as part of a linguistic table of elements, nouns she might combine to make new sentences, new ideas.

Yet, in the moment, Jamie does not combine them. She asks the noun to do its work of naming and a clarity comes from her stark syntax, from an experience teetering on the ineffable. Later, she will write of this experience, the ineffable pushing her toward sentences. It's a movement familiar, instinctive even, to writers: find yourself within a moment of unsustainable speechlessness, turn away, and then, later, try to find the words. Writing teachers have a term for that, too, one that comes from ancient Roman rhetoricians: *inventio*. For the Romans, it wasn't inventing something out of nothing but finding something that already exists (like Jamie's elementary nouns) and putting it to use.

I, too, seek these moments. Last winter, my feet in the sand, I watched waves taller than I roll onto a southern California beach. I'm six feet, eight inches. I thought of my brother who, years ago, was caught in a rip tide. He later wrote a poem with an understated first line: "I'd say the ocean is big." Drawn as I am to the water, I know I best not enter. I want to touch this leviathan but as I reach out my hand I hesitate. I proclaim the mystery. I wait.

After a two-hour drive to the ferry terminal, an hour waiting to board, a ninety-minute crossing, an hour in the harbor gathering supplies (water, lunch, dog treats), a thirty-minute drive, and a short hike, my dog and I arrive at Lime Kiln State Park. This is my routine. The trip is familiar. I name islands as we pass them. I keep this practice once, maybe twice, a year. Seeing a whale is unlikely, but my chances are better here on the water than anywhere else.

I set up at a picnic table looking west, a strong current pulling kayakers and driftwood south. In the kelp beds below the bluff, I see an occasional seal and, farther out, numerous harbor porpoise. There's a visitors' center nearby, and a large group of third graders are here on a field trip. (We all rode the ferry together, two school busses full of them.) They are divided into three groups—J-, K-, and L-pods, named for the local orcas—and while one pod is in the lighthouse, another meets with a park ranger to learn about erosion while the third hikes to the lime quarry. They rotate every thirty minutes. Soon a wedding party arrives in a black Cadillac. A bride and her four bridesmaids walk the trail, followed by her groom flanked by his four groomsmen, and, behind them all, two photographers. The bride and groom perch on some boulders, the photographer waiting for a barge to move out of his frame.

I pour water into a bowl for my dog, and we spend three hours on the bluff, my dog sunning herself while I scan the water. Nothing. We walk to the lighthouse after the L-pod kids leave, and I talk with the volunteer there. He's been charting whale sightings at Lime Kiln now twenty years. I turn a whale rib over in my hands and eye a scapula as big as a coffee table—both are part of a hands-on exhibit in the lighthouse—and the volunteer mentions a gray whale was seen off the island's southern end earlier in the day.

My dog and I leave. We drive some twelve miles south along the water, park, and walk through grasslands to another bluff, this one much higher than Lime Kiln. A bald eagle sits atop an abandoned lighthouse. I see another seal and more porpoise but no whales. We venture down the cliff and walk along the rocky shore. I'm tempted to look at the thatched and gooseneck barnacles, the sea anemones, the crabs, and the seaweed, but then I remember *If You Want to See a Whale* and turn, again, to the water. Still, no whales.

The next day we rise early and make our way to Whidbey Island, driving over Deception Pass, through forest and farmland to a remote beach that looks west toward Victoria. Six weeks ago, a juvenile gray washed ashore here, emaciated. If I'm unable to find live whales in the water, I think, then at least I can look at a dead one on the beach.

The tide is out. The beach is covered in large rocks, and I realize it's going to be a slow trek. I keep my dog on leash. If we find the whale, I do not want her messing with it. I imagine it would be near impossible to get whale out of her fur. To our left is a hundred-foot cliff, to our right the sea, and ahead, miles down the coast, Fort Ebey. We walk toward it, stopping every few hundred yards to scan water and beach, looking for whales. I do my best to keep my eyes toward the water but my mind wanders. I think of the child my friend will soon adopt, my mother's declining health, my own son now standing on his own. We keep walking. I'm wearing heavy rubber boots to protect from what we may find at the whale. We pass a few pallets washed ashore, more flotsam, and then, farther down, a driftwood hut. We keep walking. It's warm. I take off my coat, stuff it in my bag, drink some water, pour some in a bowl for my dog, and continue down the beach.

No whale yet seen, we come upon a man walking toward us. He's wearing a black jean jacket, drinking a Coke and smoking a cigarette, and hugging the cliff, milling about in the driftwood. He tells me he's out here for his "weekly therapy." "Good to get away from the city," he says and takes a drag. He pets my dog, and then I ask, "Have you seen a whale on the beach?" He just stares at me.

I explain that one washed ashore and I was hoping to find it, take a few pictures, see how big it is, and (I don't say this to him) touch it. "No, I've not seen it. If there was one here, I'd have to bring my wife out. She loves that sort of thing." I'm not sure what *that sort of thing* would be, or how a dead whale on a beach might be it, but it seems I love that sort of thing too. We talk a bit more about things found on beaches—garbage; shipwrecks; in British Columbia, the occasional human foot in a shoe—but then we return to whales. "You know," he tells me, "there are all sorts of scavengers on the beach. All those tiny crabs and shit. And there's the birds too, and the coyotes. I bet they all had a feast on that whale, ate the whole damn thing. And you can see how high the tide comes here." He points to the waterline on the cliff.

"Thanks," I say. I turn north and begin the three-mile walk back to the car. I take my dog off leash. There's no whale to worry about. The sea took it back.

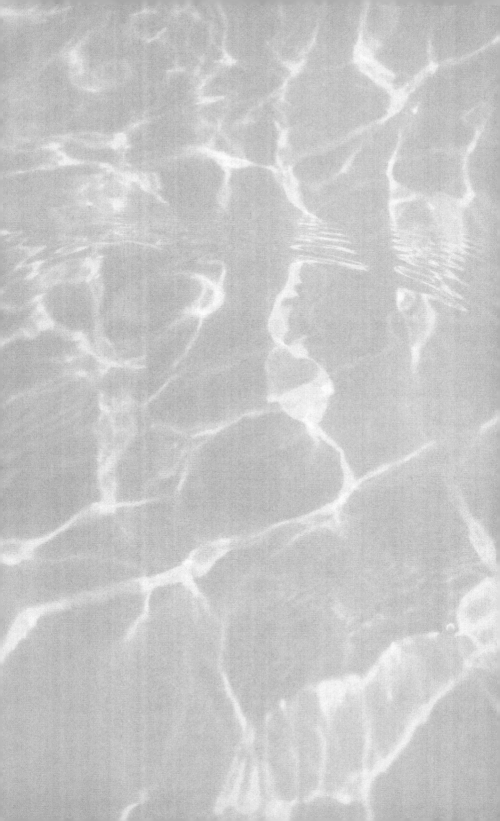

"Why do you need binoculars?" a neighbor asks. "Whales are pretty big, aren't they?"

A few weeks later, a friend suggests we go to a nearby park. "There might be whales there," he says. Walking over, I share how my favorite part of whale watching from the shore is that I rarely see them. This doesn't make sense to my friend. Since whales are wild, I tell him, and since they go wherever they please, and since the ocean is so large, we most likely won't see any. But this adds to their mystery and makes it all the more spectacular when—rather, if—we do see one.

At the park is a pair of coin-operated binoculars perched atop a four-foot metal pipe. I hand mine over to my friend, plug in a quarter, and we start looking. In the distance, two spouts.

My son has yet to adjust to the time change, and so we are awake at 4:00 a.m., his mother asleep in the hotel room. We make our way past feral cats and chickens to the boardwalk. I am barefoot and have him strapped to my chest. It's balmy. We walk down to the shore. I see something small and black rise above the water. *It's a seal*, I think, but then it gets bigger, and bigger still, and even bigger yet, and I see it is not a seal but a whale's snout and, soon, a whale's entire body, hurled from the water and crashing down again.

An orca surfaces off our stern. She wheezes. This is Granny, said to be somewhere between 80 and 101 years old, matriarch of the J-pod. With her is Spieden, along with Onyx, a twenty-year-old whose mother died when he was twelve and who has since been adopted by Granny. Had she not brought him into her pod, he would have died. Orcas are not meant to live alone.

The fog clears and we no longer see land. Our captain has taken us to a feeding ground frequented by big whales. I am the first to sight the minke. Its gray-blue back rises above the water. It dives, surfaces a second time, then is gone. We begin the two-hour voyage back to shore.

From our porch on Maui, I watch a dozen humpback whale breaches over ninety seconds. I cannot tell whether it is a dozen whales or a smaller group breaching again and again and again. Through my binoculars, the whales are gray, their splashes gray, the hillsides and sky gray too.

My wife and I drive to Lime Kiln. It's raining. We approach a bearded man in a yellow parka and hip waders. Clipboard in hand, he radios another biologist at the island's southern end, both tracking L-pod.
    "When will the whales be here?" I ask.
    The scientist glares at me. "We're not at SeaWorld."

I often search "Washington whale" online, curious what's happening in local waters, and I see that the constellation Cetus will soon be in the night sky. The cosmic whale, too, is elusive, only visible (in full) during a few winter months, parts visible (if at all) the rest of the year. Though Cetus is not the kind of whale I was looking for, I check the weather forecast for the next clear evening.

Standing in the sand, I watch a humpback breach. I glance around me, at the people sitting on beach and lawn, others lounging around the pool on the boardwalk's other side. They're all looking down at their screens.

We spent the night at Roche Harbor and are now sailing down the western side of San Juan Island. My dad has seen orcas many times in these waters. Today they stay at a distance, out on the horizon. We can see their dorsal fins, their spouts too, but they come no closer.

The ferry slows as it turns into Friday Harbor. We see a gray whale spout, its arched back breaking the water. My friend takes pictures. The whale, later identified as CRCID-30, dives. We run to the stern and see the whale surface near a fishing boat. My friend raises his camera again. I look on through my binoculars.

On a pier in Santa Barbara someone yells, "Whale!" I run to the railing, look down, and see a gray whale calf circling below. The mother is nowhere in sight. A crowd gathers.

When my wife is pregnant, I have a recurring dream. I am walking the beach. An orca calf washes ashore. I come to its side and, delirious, try to roll it back to the sea. People soon restrain me, pulling me back from the dead whale, and a man tells me, "Sometimes nature takes back its young."

On Whidbey Island overlooking the Admiralty Inlet, I see a few harbor porpoise, a sea lion, and then, a humpback. My companions cannot see it without binoculars. The whale dives for two to three minutes then surfaces again, its angular hump cresting. The whale cruises, back and forth, back and forth, in front of the same stretch of beach on the far side of the channel.

I'd spent two hours that afternoon scanning the water before sighting that whale. *Persistence pays off,* I think. But when I tell a colleague about it, he says he's been walking that same stretch of beach, back and forth, back and forth, fourteen years and has never seen a whale.

That same afternoon, I meet two biologists from local universities. They're taking a census of marine life in the channel. So when I see the humpback, I run across the bluff to tell them. We three raise our binoculars. I mention that I regularly listen to the livestream hydrophone off Lime Kiln State Park. "That makes me happy," the lead biologist says. "I'm the guy who installed it."

My wife, son, and I are on the boardwalk, returning from viewing a sperm whale skeleton, when we see a crowd gathered, phones up, waiting. "There are whales here," one of them tells us. Before I can remove my lens cover a humpback breaches. It's close enough I can see the white of its belly, the green, brown, and orange barnacles along its snout and jaw, the deep grooves of its throat.

Off the coast of the Bell Chain Islets, some orcas come upon a rock covered with seals. The thirteen whales split, a bull staying on the rock's northern side and the other twelve swimming to its southern side. He charges, creating a wave that crashes against the seals. The seals inch over the top of the rock and down its backside, their eyes on the big orca before them and their backs toward the dozen awaiting them.

The bull then stops splashing the seals. Bored? Distracted? No longer hungry? The orcas regroup and swim away. The seals relax, as do we on the boat.

Sailing with his brother, my father sees a lone orca in the distance. It turns, now swimming toward their boat, toward its broadside, steadily, confidently, quickly, picking up speed. Scared of being stove,

38   { Interlude

by dad jumps atop the cabin and hugs the mast. Still, the whale approaches. At the last moment it dives, my uncle and father watching it swim under their keel, pectoral fins reaching wide, surfacing on the other side only to then dive again.

As we board the ferry, the man taking tickets tells us to watch for whales. "There have been a lot of sightings today. Orcas, humpbacks, everything. All in the ferry lanes."

I'm with two friends. One borrows my binoculars to look at a yacht with elliptical machines and a weight set on its roof, a wooden boat perched on its stern, and he's the first to see it. "Right there," he says, handing me the binoculars. "Straight ahead, three-quarters of the way between us and that other ferry."

I soon see it too: a minke, heading north, its black, sleek, shiny back rising above the surface, its sharp curved dorsal fin following. After five minutes, it surfaces again, still well ahead of us but now traveling south. Given the lack of interest on the ferry deck, it doesn't seem anyone else has seen the whale.

My friends ride their bikes to a beach where a whale has washed ashore. They tell me they could smell it before they could see it. The Lummi Tribe claims the whale and tows him to uninhabited Portage Island. There his flesh will rot away until the bones can be retrieved.

I am an undergraduate and not a poet, but I try writing a poem anyway—it seems a fitting gesture, necessary too, even if not done well—a poem in response to the whale, twenty-one three-line stanzas, a poem that borrows from newspaper stories covering the event, the poem my first attempt to write the whale.

> Silence please
> for the fin whale on Lummi
> found bloated and dead
>
> Four years old and not full grown
> fifty-seven feet one day he might have weighed
> one hundred thirty tons

An ocean liner
a steel behemoth
plowed into the leviathan

Walking the docks with my son in the stroller and my dog at our side, we come upon five fishermen mending their nets. They're preparing for the upcoming chum run in the Puget Sound. There's an open case of Rainier tallboys on the deck, Hendrix on a radio. One of the crew sits on an overturned five-gallon bucket. Another paces off the netting—some orange, other parts brown, some lime green, some black. He's in Carhartts and a black T-shirt; a third crew member wears a straw hat. They work on a purse seiner, the *Silver Wave*, sailing out of Bainbridge Island.

"Do whales ever swim through your nets?" I ask.

"Oh yeah," one answers, pointing to a nearby Chevy. "They make a hole the size of that truck."

"They just barrel right through?"

"That's what you want. It's a mess when they get tangled."

From the cabin someone calls out, "Remember that whale two years ago? The hole he made was ten times the size of that truck."

Ferrying from Port Townsend, I see a flock of gulls descend on the water. There is frantic activity at the surface. I assume a bait ball is beneath, the birds, perhaps seals too, feeding. Something breaches. A porpoise? No, too large, but I'm unable to tell what it was given how the splash fell. So I keep looking. Then, a dorsal fin, tall, maybe six feet, with others surrounding it, rises from the water. Orcas, a male with three females. They surface multiple times in the midst of the birds, the birds flying higher now, away from the whales. My friend and I pass the binoculars between us. The whales dive. We search but cannot find them again.

THREE } A Heap of Stones

Whales, of course, pose a great problem to the would-be
lexicographer: they are always diving down.

—Dan Beachy-Quick
A Whaler's Dictionary

In *Several Short Sentences about Writing*, a book I've taught many
times, Verlyn Klinkenborg speaks to the importance, for writers, of
naming. To write, Klinkenborg says, is to notice the world around
you and, from that noticing, find the names for what you see. These
names, he says, "announce the whatness of the world to a single
species."

But learning names, and how to use them, is hard. There are just
so many names. "This is a planet of overlapping lexicons, generation
after generation, trade after trade, expedition after expedition sent
out to bring home name upon name, terms of identity in endless
degrees of intricacy." All these names are "at hand," according to
Klinkenborg, "if you look for them."

His "if" carries a lot of weight. I read in it an admonishment that
the writer *should* look for these names, these words. Klinkenborg
continues:

Don't neglect such a rich linguistic inheritance. It's your business to
know the names of things, to recover them if necessary and use them.
This isn't merely a matter of expanding your vocabulary. It's a matter of
understanding that everything you see and know about your presence
in this moment of perception is overlaid by a parallel habitat of language, names that lie tacit until you summon them.

Though he's speaking to writers, I want to extend Klinkenborg's argument. Anyone—assuming they are verbal—cannot perceive the world, cannot make sense of it, without language, without the names for what it is that's being seen and experienced. Those names lie there, tacit, unbidden, dormant, until summoned from their sleep. We need our nouns.

"Call me Ishmael" may be the most famous first sentence in American literature, but it's actually not the first sentence of *Moby-Dick*. The book begins in a library, with a schoolmaster "threadbare in coat, heart, body, and brain." The story continues:

> I see him now. He was ever dusting his old lexicons and grammars, with a queer handkerchief, mockingly embellished with all the gay flags of all the known nations of the world. He loved to dust his old grammars; it somehow mildly reminded him of his mortality.

The as-of-yet unnamed narrator watches "the pale Usher" dote on his grammar books and dictionaries, and, as if I'm looking over the shoulder of both narrator and librarian, Melville opens those dictionaries for me and gives names for the whale:

חן,	*Hebrew.*
κητος,	*Greek.*
CETUS,	*Latin.*
WHŒL,	*Anglo-Saxon.*
HVALT,	*Danish.*
WAL,	*Dutch.*
HWAL,	*Swedish.*
WHALE,	*Icelandic.*
WHALE,	*English.*
BALEINE,	*French.*
BALLENA,	*Spanish.*
PEKEE-NUEE-NUEE,	*Fegee.*
PEHEE-NUEE-NUEE,	*Erromangoan.*

Not for another ten pages does the narrator tell me what I can call him. Ishmael gives his name only after the whale's.

Ishmael returns to names later in the novel when trying to catalogue all species of whale. He writes, "I give the popular fishermen's names for all these fish, for generally they are the best." But Ishmael is not always satisfied with these names: "Where any name happens to be vague or inexpressive, I shall say so, and suggest another." For *Black Fish*, then, Ishmael prefers Hyena Whale, since all whales look black under water, and Hyena better describes this whale's behavior. (I'm not sure how to read Ishmael's italics here. Some whale names he italicizes, others not. Whatever he's thinking, I'll retain his formatting on these names.) The *Narwhale*, he notes, could also be called the *Nostril Whale*, "his peculiar horn being originally mistaken for a peaked nose." Some call it the *Hump Back* whale, others call it the Elephant and Castle whale. The *Fin-Back* could be called the Tall-Spout or the Long John. The *Sperm Whale* is also called the Tumpa whale, the Physeter, the Anvil Headed whale, the Cachalot, the Pottfisch, or the Macrocephalus. The *Right Whale*, Ishmael notes, "is indiscriminately designated by the all the following titles: The Whale; the Greenland Whale; the Black Whale; the Great Whale; the True Whale; the Right Whale."

I question Ishmael's use of "indiscriminate." These names are not inconsequential. There's a reason for each. The *Sulphur Bottom*, Ishmael tells readers, gets its name from its "brimstone" belly, yellowed from diving so deep as to scrape the roof of hell. Or consider the *Razor Back*. Ishmael notes, "Of this whale little is known but his name." Ishmael can call it, he can name it, he can label it for the sake of classification—but that's it. "He has never yet shown any part of him but his back, which rises in a long sharp ridge." *Sulphur Bottom*, *Razor Back*, these—and all other whale names—cling to what little is known so that one might reach for the ineffable.

In an essay reflecting on his own name and the people he shares it with, Ander Monson claims, "We project our myths on names." The name becomes shorthand for a story—real, imagined, hearsay, longed for, dreaded. A sailor sees something in the water, can't identify it, and so names it after its razor back. Days, months, years later, and this animal carries a story with it, carries with it a narrative, a narrative that is rewritten with each encounter it has with humans. The name becomes a myth while creating it, a myth colored by all previous interactions, a myth that then shapes the sailor's response to that whale, furthering the mythology around it. It's a feedback loop.

Philip Hoare never misses an opportunity to talk etymology. Throughout his book *The Whale*, he pauses, again and again, to say something of a whale's name. It's a quick way to introduce readers to animals they've likely never seen. The name shares a bit of the whale's past. Hoare's main purpose in the book isn't etymology—he's obsessed with *Moby-Dick*, and *The Whale* reads as a companion to it, even appropriating Melville's chapter titles for its own—but etymologies are vital to his project. It's a subtle argument on Hoare's part: humans cannot know whales, or begin to know whales, until we know what we can call them. Names come first.

Hear these names and the stories they tell, all from Hoare: whalers nicknamed the humpback "the merry whale, although its scientific name is hardly less glamourous: *Megaptera novæangliæ*, big-winged New Englander, barnacled angel." *Rorqual*—a blanket term for large baleen whales—comes "from the Scandinavian for reed or furrowed whale, a reference to their ridged bellies." These terms are descriptive, like the Latin for sperm whale, "classified as *Physter macrocephalus* or 'big-headed blower' by Linnæus." The blue whale, too: "Even Linnæus's name for it is a little Swedish joke: *Balænoptera musculus*—*Balæna* meaning whale, *pteron*, wing or fin, and *musculus*, both muscular, and mouse." Or the pilot whale, "so called because they followed a leader." Because of right whales' "propensity to hug the shoreline," they're called "the urban whale." "Beluga, or belukhas . . . owe their common name to the Russian for white, *belyy*. . . . Sailors called them canaries of the sea on account of their songs." The narwhal gets its name "from the Old Norse, *nar* and *hvalr*, meaning 'corpse whale,' because its smudges resemble the livid blemishes on a dead body." And, "Grey whales were called devil fish for their propensity to turn on their hunters." Baleen whales, together, are called mysticetes, from the Latin *mystax*, meaning "moustached whales."

But for all these names and the stories they tell, Hoare reminds readers of something important: "That in oceans swim great whales unnamed by man."

Ander Monson continues, thinking now about the memories wrapped up within a name. "My response," he writes, "to a Timothy, say, is colored by all the previous Timothys I have known, that I may have disliked intensely, so Timothy is a name, too timorous and obtuse to get very far in life, of people that I am more likely to dislike." Monson knows names are freighted with history. Anyone who's tried to name a child has run into this Timothy problem.

I came at it another way. Rather than cut potential names because of the memories they conjure, I added more to the list—Gustav, Emma Louise, Adelia, Hieronymus, Ballard, Rainier—each an opportunity to revisit the past, an opportunity to tell a story. I asked my wife if she might consider giving our son not one but three middle names. Each one, I suggested, is a placeholder for a larger story. We can pass down family history through these names.

A few years ago a friend named his son after me. It seemed fitting, then, to name our son after him, one of those many middle names. When we did, he sent a letter. He wrote of names as "reminders," as, he called them, "Ebenezers." He quoted from the Old Testament— "Then Samuel took a stone and set it up between Mizpah and Shen and called its name Ebenezer"—and then explained that "Ebenezer means 'stone of help.' You see the Israelites doing similar things all throughout their life as a nation: setting up reminders that the Lord continues to be sure help, that he has brought them this far." I need these reminders, these names and the stories they tell, these heaps of stones.

The sperm whale got its name because whalers thought the thick milky material in its forehead was the whale's sperm. In spring 2018, one showed up in Johnstone Strait, between Vancouver Island and

British Columbia. It made its presence known—rather, heard—before being seen. Researchers tracked it acoustically for days before finally snapping the verifying photo. Not since 1984 had one been in the area.

An acquaintance sent a recording she made of it: thirty-four minutes of what sounds like a nail gun, again and again, penetrating the deep. Whalers sometimes called the sperm whale the "grey-headed whale" for the "pepper and salt color of his head." It was also called the cachalot, from the Basque for *tooth*, as it is the largest of the toothed whales and the only of the great whales to have teeth rather than baleen. Another name for it: the carpenter whale, for how its sonar sounds on the hulls of wooden ships. A sperm whale can stun, even kill, its prey with these sound waves. I put the recording on repeat. We each carry on our respective day's work, the carpenter whale hammering away while I read and write.

Then there's the right whale: it swims close to shore, is slow, floats when dead, and has an abundance of blubber. It was the *right* whale to hunt. Just as the right whale is named by an industry that hunted it to near extinction, so too the sperm whale's name reflects the use of spermaceti for cosmetics, leatherworking, and lubricants. We made crayons of these animals, washed our bodies in soaps from their fats, lit our streetlamps with their oils. Margarine, pet food, vitamins, ice cream, brake oil, grease for frying food, glue, shoe soles, insulin, medicines, corsets, umbrellas, plant food. During my undergraduate years, I studied in a library reading room with whale-skin doors.

The sperm whale's and right whale's names both derive from their exploitation. They "are named for their usefulness to man." These names are a far cry from the Greek for whale, *ketos*, which means sea monster. Cetology and cetacean derive from it, and the narrative of fear, of mystery, of monstrosity in *ketos* is absent in names like sperm and right whale, names of utility, of extraction, of commerce, of capitalism.

I think, too, of the killer whale. Whalers coined the name *whale killer* in response to how ferocious this whale is (the name later inverted). Its scientific name—*Orcinus orca*—also conjures death. *Orca* is Latin for "a kind of whale" and *orcinus* translates to "of or belonging to the realms of the dead." Orcus is also the name of a Roman god of the underworld. No surprise, then, that its nickname, at one time, was demon dolphin.

Of all these names for the killer whale—they're also called blackfish, and grampus—I'm partial to wolves of the sea. It resonates with a story the Siberian Yupik tell. They call the orca *aarlug*, and the *aarlug* and wolf are the same animal. The *aarlug* comes ashore in winter to become the wolf and in summer returns to the sea to become whale once again. The roots of this myth: both are black and white, both live and hunt and travel in matriarchal packs and pods, both are apex predators, one of the sea, the other of the land. All this told by *aarlug*.

In 2012, in a mom-and-pop used bookstore in Pittsburgh, I found a copy of Reginald B. Hegarty's *Returns of Whaling Vessels Sailing from American Ports, 1876–1928*. It's a thin green book with a gilded title, hardbound, pages brittle and yellowed, cracking, smelling not of sea but of cellar. For its fifty-eight pages I paid $45.

Hegarty details every whaling ship—its name, rig, tons, captain, and agents—sailing out of the United States during those fifty-three years, as well as where each ship was bound, when it sailed, and when it returned (if at all). The far columns tally how many barrels of sperm oil and whale oil and pounds of whalebone each ship gathered. The final column notes any extraordinary circumstances of the voyage, and the final pages collect the average prices of whale oil each year: $1.13 per gallon in 1877 with a steady decline to $.12 per gallon in 1932.

I bring the *Returns* to class, along with a second, larger set of returns I picked up a few weeks prior at a used bookstore in Port Townsend. It was a serendipitous find. Hegarty's book has a subtitle—*A Continuation of Alexander Starbuck's "History of the American Whale Fishery"*—and what did I find in that bookstore but Alexander Starbuck's 779-page *History of the American Whale Fishery*.

In Starbuck's book, I put Post-it Notes on the pages naming ships we'd encountered already. We had been reading the diary of Annie Holmes Ricketson, entries from when she had accompanied her husband, Captain Daniel L. Ricketson, on a whaling voyage. (She was the only woman aboard.) According to Starbuck's records, their ship—the *A. R. Tucker*, classified as a bark—sailed from New Bedford on 2 May 1871 for the Indian Ocean, returning 18 October 1874 with 220 barrels of sperm oil. In the remarks column, I read the ship "Sent home 344 sperm." On 3 January 1841, I see the *Acushnet* set sail from Fairhaven under Captain Pease, headed for the Pacific. Built in 1840, this is her maiden voyage (years later she'll lose six men when a whale stove one of her boats), and she returned home 13 May 1845 with 850 barrels of sperm oil, 1,350 barrels of whale-oil, and 13,500 pounds of whalebone. Herman Melville was aboard. I've also marked the *Essex*, sailing for the Pacific under Captain George Pollard Jr. and leaving from Nantucket on 12 August 1819. In the remarks column: "Stove by a whale November, 1820; captain, mate, and three men saved in the boats; three men left on Disco Island." This is the event—right here, documented in the returns—that inspired *Moby-Dick*.

Students are surprised by the precision in the returns, data presented in clean rows and columns giving a sense of reality to what we've been reading together. These aren't just fish stories told by an ancient mariner. They're stories verified by the names, barrels, pounds, and remarks columns. That we can look up a whaling ship—any ship sailing from 1784 through 1928—gives a materiality to these stories. I can run my finger along the returns, touch these pages and their ink, and wonder.

I ask my students what they notice about Hegarty's and Starbuck's books. This is a question I ask often—*what do you notice?*—an effort to habituate students to pay attention to what they notice and, once they see something, to find the words to name it. They're quick to note the small font. One student wants a magnifying glass, a technology that's obsolete now, she says, with so many people reading on screens.

Another mentions that the books chronicle death. Death is meticulously counted, measured, weighed, catalogued, and documented. The *Swallow* docked in New Bedford on 10 April 1887 with 8,000 pounds of whalebone; the *Monticello*, sailing from Provincetown over to the Pacific Ocean, returned with a meager five barrels of sperm oil but 19,700 pounds of whale bone; the *Ann Maria*, at sea a little under two years, returned home 5 March 1841 with seventy barrels of sperm oil; the *Mars*, captained by W. H. Robinson and sailing from San Francisco in 1890, managed, in nine months, to take only a single whale.

One student notices how the books are organized. "It's all set up around the names of the boats," she says. She's right. Within each year, ships are listed alphabetically under the port they sailed from. Starbuck and Hegarty could have arranged these returns by each ship's yields, or by the dates the ships set sail, or by each ship's size, but no—they chose to write history by names.

Every ship name in the book carries a narrative, and the stories told by these names are tragedies of mutiny, of hurricane, of ships lost at sea or condemned at port. Sailing out of Warren, Rhode Island, in 1839, the *North America* "lost several of the crew by scurvy." The *Inga* "returned in consequence of a leak" on 23 December 1847. The *Superior*, sailing out of New Bedford in 1857, was "Burned by natives of Solomon Islands, and all but 6 of the crew massacred." In 1868, the *S. N. Smith*, sailing under Captain Rounseville, never returned, "the captain's wife, 2 children, first and second mates, boat-steerers, and 13 of the crew lost." The *Abram Barker*, sailing out of San Francisco in 1893, was lost at Cape Navarin on 7 May 1894, the crew saved by the *Horatio*, captained by E. B. Penniman. There is the *Draco*—I assume named after the dragon slain by Hercules, a poignant name given the ship's own slaying of leviathans—condemned at St. Helena in 1880, and the *Petrel*, lost with fifteen men aboard after only three days at sea. The *A. R. Tucker*—the same ship Miss Ricketson traveled on from 1871 to 1874 and whose journals we'd read—later sailed out of New Bedford on 6 June 1899, and saw its captain, M. Millard, die at sea. "Command taken by 1st Mate Bento," the returns tell me, and as the sentence continues, I notice his change in title, and his unfortunate fate: "Capt. Bento killed by a whale."

These logs list hundreds upon hundreds of such entries, and the expendable parties—the whales, and the working-class sailors too—have no individual names. Both are disposable and readily replaced. There is no acknowledgement, no suggestion that one whale might be unique from another. A sperm whale is a sperm whale is a sperm whale, with no story unto itself other than the shared narrative of whaling. These whalers did not yet know that humpbacks can be differentiated one from another by the white splotches under their flukes unique to each whale; orcas by the saddle patches behind their notched dorsal fins; grays by patterns of scarring, barnacles, and mottling on their flanks; fin whales by scars left from ship strikes. From these marks, researchers can now track individual whales, construct a narrative of a life, follow one through childhood, puberty, adulthood, and—if an orca—menopause, such research made possible by the individuation a name offers, such individuation absent in the logs.

I cannot think of any other animal—save for the fish, which itself is a sloppy term for *whale*—whose name tells of its own demise, the name a narrative of death, a narrative told in so many parts of speech: a verb (to whale), a noun (whaler), and a participle, gerund, and adjective (whaling). The whaler assumes the name of his prey, the two becoming one.

Richard Poirier writes that language can bring one to a "point of vibrant intersection" with the unknown—in Thoreau's case, a field of beans; in mine, whales—and I want to think that naming this leviathan could bring me there, situate me within that field. Yet I hesitate to rely on names too much. "What does one do with the whale brought up on its wordy-hook?" Dan Beachy-Quick asks. "Catch and release and let the beast dive back into the unfathomable region that makes its name a question, or kill it and see what it is you 'know.'"

That's what happens, the name familiarizing the unknown, pulling it closer even as it swims away. I think of this each time I say *whale*, the name itself an attempt to explain away the unknown.

And so, I am trying to change how I say *whale*, no longer pronouncing it as *wail* but drawing out the *h*. The result is a voiceless *wh* that pours into a voiced *ale*, an exhalation not unlike the draft that escapes a whale's blowhole. I hear this pronunciation as a sound-image that mirrors, or at least attempts to with my feeble lungs, the breathing of the leviathan. It's an effort to breathe some life into a name that has become, perhaps, too familiar.

Before Melville gives those thirteen translations of whale, he quotes Richard Hackluyt on the *h*: "While you take in hand to school others, and to teach them by what name a whale-fish is to be called in our tongue, leaving out, through ignorance, the letter H, which almost alone maketh up the signification of the word, you deliver that which is not true." The reason the *h* is so important, the reason its absence distorts the whale, is that *h* is at the root of the Swedish and Danish for whale: *hval*. Melville points to *Webster's Dictionary*: "This animal is named from roundness or rolling; for in Dan. *Hvalt* is arched or vaulted." The *h* is, as Beachy-Quick would say, "The sound in which one dwells"; it is what brings me into the word. I exhale, and through that breath, voice *whale*.

Teaching myself to say *whale* anew, I recall a poem my friend sent to mark the moment he named his son after me. The poem is by Anne Ridler, and she's writing about naming her own son. Her words seem oddly appropriate now as I try to relearn the leviathan's name, as I try to inhabit this word:

> I give, though ignorant for whom
> The history and power of a name.
> I conjure with it, like a novice
> Summoning unknown spirits: answering me
> You take the word, and tame it.

I doubt I can, or ever will, "tame" this name. Though I know the etymology of *hval*, I am ignorant the power of the name, its full history. We are all ignorant, despite our best efforts. I say *whale*, and I conjure unknown spirits, summon unknown stories. Ridler continues:

> You take the famous name you did not choose
> And make it new.

She's speaking to her son, of him adding his own story to the history of a name—a name he did not get to choose for himself—but I read these lines with me as their "you," taking *whale*—this famous name I did not choose but inherited—and attempting to make it new.

> You and the name exchange a power:
>   Its history is changed, becoming yours,
>   And yours by this: who calls this, calls you.

I want my students to learn how to say *whale*. I'm not sure I even know how to say it, or what I summon when I say the name, or even the whatness I'm announcing when I utter these sounds. But we will learn together.

When reading research on whales, or stories about them, I hear an inflection to the word, a certain way people who know whales write about them, talk about them, think about them that carries through their sentences. They've learned how to use the word, and they've learned what it means—and how—to say it. They know what stories the name carries within it, the stories the name conjures.

I hear this inflection in the following paragraph, from Kathleen Jamie's essay "The Hvalsalen," a piece in which she visits the University of Bergen's Natural History Museum and finds a twenty-four-meter whale skeleton.

> Of course, the blue whale was largest of all. I decided to walk under its full length, and count my steps. First, I walked under the smooth horizontal arch of the jaw, and its palate, where the baleen had once hung, sheets of age-browned bone. Then came the solid complications of the skull, now under the barrel of the rib cage, the ribs curving down, enclosing nothing but air. I kept walking, counting. As I passed the basking shark I surreptitiously touched its cold skin, rough as sandpaper. I

passed a dolphin, small and lithe, and making for the door. Still the blue whale went on overhead. Above the basking shark hung a huge sunfish, an eerie-looking object hanging from a wire, more like a black moon with an eye. Still I walked on, counting until the spine ended. Fifty-seven paces. Less an animal, more a narrative. The ancient mariner.

I ask my students what they notice about this paragraph. "Still," one says immediately. "Jamie repeats it a lot. She's walking, still walking, and still walking." I ask what purpose that *still* serves, what its job is. "It's for a sense of scale," a student in the back says. She explains that *still* situates Jamie in relation to the whale above her. It gives a sense of movement to the prose. Another student notices how many other animals are mentioned in the passage, and he speculates that these operate the same way *still* does. They tell readers the whale is so large it has four other bodies—basking shark, dolphin, sunfish, and Jamie herself—beneath it. Jamie knows how to say *whale*, and as my students have shown me, it comes, in part, through sentences that place her and others in relation to it.

I wonder what fifty-seven paces looks like. As our discussion continues, I pace the classroom, counting steps in my head. For a moment, I think of telling my students that Jamie's whale is roughly four times the length of this room we're in—but then I remember the old writing adage "show, don't tell." It would be better for them to see these fifty-seven paces themselves.

We grab our coats, push through the double doors, head to a nearby road, and gather under a lamppost. I ask a student to walk Jamie's fifty-seven paces. As she begins, the fifteen of us, standing in the rain, guess how far these fifty-seven paces will take her. She calls out every ten steps, passing some shrubs, two flower beds, and a few more lampposts along her way. We soon realize our predictions are all well short.

A few weeks later, in response to Kathleen Jamie walking under that blue whale skeleton, a student writes that Jamie "taught me perspective." I wonder about the use of "perspective" here. I think back to a moment in elementary school when, in art class, I learned what foreshortening means. To create the appearance of depth on a sheet of paper, I could draw objects close to the viewer larger and objects farther away smaller. With Jamie, perspective comes when we see the whale in relation to her. A reader knows how large a human is and how long a stride is. Setting the whale against these gives "perspective."

The student continues. Reading Jamie "taught me perspective, as did physically walking out the paces of the length of the whale described in the essay." For this student, it's not enough to read about the whale, not enough to imagine what it must be like to walk fifty-seven paces. No, it's the "physically walking" that gives perspective. This knowledge is embodied. The student finds perspective only once her body is engaged, her legs moving, her muscles contracting, her lungs inhaling and exhaling, her shoulders wet from the rain.

I note, too, her syntax, the way she piles on preposition after preposition after preposition: "*out* the paces *of* the length *of* the whale described *in* the essay." Perspective comes through grammar. Just as Jamie sets herself against the whale to create perspective, the student's sentence sets "walking" alongside "paces" alongside "length" alongside "whale" alongside "essay" to do the same. The sentence reaches across the page as Jamie's whale does the room. Perhaps the student is imitating Jamie's use of *still*. Jamie repeats the word to give a sense of the whale's length; the student heaps on prepositional phrases to do the same.

That heaping, though, means the sentence is not as lean as it might be: "as did physically walking out the paces of the length of the whale described in the essay" could be much shorter. "physically" isn't necessary (is there any way to walk but physically?), and those prepositional phrases could be tightened up too, into something like this: "as did walking the whale's length." There. Six words instead of seventeen. One-third the length. But something is lost in this economy—the sense of movement, the sense of length, the sense of exhaustion at striding along, step after step after step, preposition after preposition after preposition, trying to reach the end of that fifty-seven-pace whale. The plodding prepositions are not extraneous to this sentence but essential to it. The sentence works because it's ungainly. Very like a whale.

When I read "as did physically walking out the paces of the length of the whale described in the essay," I hear in it the inflection on *whale* I hear in Jamie's sentences. Walking the whale has brought this student to an awareness of what she summons when she utters its name. Here she raises her Ebenezer, the whale's name a reminder of that walking, of those paces, of the perspective given her.

FOUR } An Inheritance

The profound skepticism of our age, the mistrust of all that has been
handed to us by our grandfathers and grandmothers as tradition, has
led to a curious failure of the imagination, manifested in language that
is thoroughly comfortable, and satisfyingly unchallenging.
                                                    —Kathleen Norris
                                Amazing Grace: A Vocabulary of Faith

During the winter of 2012 I memorized the Book of Jonah. I was
prompted by *Fahrenheit 451*—the book about a world that burns
books—by a scene wherein a group of exiles gathers. They've each
memorized books, and one tells another, "*You are* the Book of
Ecclesiastes." I am drawn to this idea of internalizing then becoming
a text, making the words part of your own being, such that the text
lives on—lives through—your engagement with it.

Each day followed the same routine. Recite the previous day's
verse ten times from memory. Recite the current day's verse ten
times with the text in front of me. Recite it again, ten times, without
the text, and then, as the capstone to the day's work, recite what I
had of the book thus far. Doing this, I memorized Jonah's forty-eight
verses in six weeks.

I now recite the book aloud daily, once, sometimes twice, often
more. I figure I've done it upward of some 3,500 times. It takes eight
minutes. When my mind is unoccupied the verses come involun-
tarily. They become mileposts for my day, marking its progression
as I recite during my morning walk with my dog, my walk to work,
my bus rides around town, my walk home, my evening walk with my
dog. Whenever I am near water—on a boat, or walking the docks,

or at a beach—I recite it. Seems fitting, necessary even, to tell an old fish story when by the sea.

When I was writing my dissertation, my adviser told me every good thing he'd ever written began with him sitting at his desk with three or four passages from books he'd copied onto sheets of paper. A writer's job, he said, was to figure out how to make those passages speak to each other. The etymology of *composition* is important here: *com-* a prefix meaning "together," and *position* a variation of the Latin *ponere*, "to place." A placing together. Saying something new isn't a matter of inventing ideas from scratch but of composing those gathered.

And to compose, a writer must work with words handed down. Here's how David Bartholomae, a figure well known among writing teachers, describes it. He's discussing the challenge of learning to use words and, through that usage, find yourself in them. "The language is not yours," he writes, "You did not invent it; it is not yours and yet, ironically, it is one of the most crucial ways you have of being present—of being present in the world, in the workplace, in the academy." Bartholomae argues learning to write means learning to understand words as passed down, as situated within "history, expectation, desire, and convention." That is, a writer inherits words and then must compose them, must ask them to do certain kinds of work, work the writer knows these words can do based on how they've been used in the past and, too, work the writer knows may stretch the capabilities of these words. And the way to learn this—"the most effective lesson," Bartholomae says—"is to get inside and to work inside sentences."

For Herman Melville, the work is slow. This, from a letter sent while composing *Moby-Dick*:

> About the "whaling voyage"—I am half way in the work, & am very glad that your suggestion so jumps with mine. It will be a strange sort of a

book, tho', I fear; blubber is blubber you know; tho' you may get oil out of it, the poetry runs as hard as sap from a frozen maple tree;—& to cook the thing up, one must needs throw in a little fancy, which from the nature of the thing, must be ungainly as the gambols of the whales themselves.

It's strange, this way Melville writes of his writing. He's on the boat himself, on a whaling voyage, extracting oil from blubber, the poetry running hard and slow. He's loading blubber into the try-pots, rendering it down to oil, laboring to turn this unrefined resource into something consumable. He is writing.

Nowhere is this more evident than in the Extracts that open *Moby-Dick*, the seventy-nine quotations Melville presents in the first nine pages of his book. They come right after Melville lists *whale* in thirteen languages. The Extracts are the sap from the tree, the extracted blubber that must be processed, the raw material Melville will turn into his masterpiece. These passages come from all over, each touching upon whales in some way, Melville quoting from Genesis, Job, Jonah, the Psalms, Isaiah, *Paradise Lost, The Faerie Queen* (as he spells it), *Hamlet*, whalers' logs, poetry, letters, fiction, *Thomas Beale's History of the Sperm Whale*, Darwin, whaling songs, missionaries' journals, political philosophy, even a report of a speech to the US Senate, and more.

He reads like a pirate, pillaging from wherever he can. If there is any meaning to be made here, it comes not from Melville—he presents each extract without commentary—but from how the Extracts speak to each other, through how they are composed, their juxtaposition highlighting the many facets of the whale. And so Melville presents this passage, from Isaiah,

> In that day, the Lord with his sore, and great, and strong sword, shall punish Leviathan the piercing serpent, even Leviathan that crooked serpent; and he shall slay the dragon that is in the sea.

Alongside this, from *Sir William Davenant's Preface to Gondibert*,

> Immense as whales, the motion of whose vast bodies can in a peaceful calm trouble the ocean till it boil.

Alongside this, from *Paradise Lost*,

That sea beast
Leviathan, which God of all his works
Created hugest that swim the ocean stream.

Alongside this, from *Cooper's Pilot*,

"No, Sir, 'tis a Right Whale," answered Tom; "I saw his spout; he threw
up a pair of as pretty rainbows as a Christian would wish to look at.
He's a raal oil-butt, that fellow!"

Alongside this, from *John Hunter's account of the dissection of a
whale (a small sized one)*,

Ten or fifteen gallons of blood are thrown out of the heart at a stroke,
with immense velocity.

Alongside this, from *Scoresby*,

The quantity of line withdrawn from the different boats engaged in
the capture of this one whale, amounted altogether to 10,400 yards or
nearly six English miles.

And so on, and so on. Melville discards nothing. He is exhaustively
thorough. He's working to include all he can about this animal he at
once knows so much about and yet so little. But the Extracts, in their
breadth, read as incomplete. Their reach implies there's still more out
there. Melville could keep gathering whale passages, the only thing
stopping him his readers' expectation that he should get going with
the story. *Moby-Dick* is, after all, a novel.

While Melville was writing *Moby-Dick*, "friends began to call
books to his attention and to send him choice little passages about
whales that went into his 'Extracts.'" I look at my own bookshelves
laden with whale trinkets gifted me, and I look at my reading list for
this book, much of it coming through recommendations of friends,
family, students, teachers, and colleagues. I read the Extracts as rec-
ognizing people—in Melville's life and my own—an acknowledgment
that reading and writing happen within community, others handing
me and him these words to compose.

The reverend asks me and my wife if we have "a verse to give" our son at his baptism. I am not entirely sure what it means to give someone a verse. I recall a poetry reading, months before, when the poet said, "I have these poems for you tonight"—his words a gift, something handed from one person to another, something to be treasured even. Giving a verse to our son, I come to think, means it will be over him his entire life. A blessing of sorts, a prophecy perhaps. We choose to give him the first line from Jonah's prayer in the belly of the whale:

> I called out to the Lord, out of my distress,
>   and he answered me.

Giving these words, I wonder whether they will be true for him. He's six weeks old at his baptism, and quiet at the moment, but I know he will soon be in distress—if not immediately, then surely within the hour. He will call out, for his mother to nurse him, for me to change him, for us to love him. And we will answer that call. I hope, as he grows, his calls are always answered.

As I memorize the Book of Jonah, as I become familiar with the prophet's words, as they work into my imagination, that verse stands out to me not only for its narrative of rescue, but also because I've seen it elsewhere. I begin hearing resonances between Jonah's prayer and various Psalms I encounter here and there, the two playing off each other. Consider the first verse of Jonah's prayer—the one we gave our son—against this, from Psalm 120:

> In my distress I called to the Lord,
>   and he answered me.

I'm inclined to think this a coincidence. Lots of prophets call to the Lord in their distress. That's what prophets do. But as I continue working through Jonah, I start to suspect this prophet's words are not his own. The next bit of his prayer (on the left), set alongside a verse from Psalm 86:

| Out of the belly of Sheol I cried, | You have delivered my soul from the depths |
| and you heard my voice. | of Sheol. |

Sheol appears often in the Hebraic scriptures—one translator refers to it as "a shadowy realm of nonbeing into which the dead descend"—and deliverance from Sheol is a common trope. These are stock sentences, Jonah using the common language of his faith. Here is the next verse of Jonah's prayer, which I'll set alongside verses from Psalms 69 and 42:

For you cast me into the deep,
    into the heart of the seas,
    and the flood surrounded me;
All your waves and your billows
    passed over me.
	Save me, O God!
	    For the waters have come up to my neck.
	
	All your breakers and your waves
	    have gone over me.

These vast, unmeasured, boundless, free waters roll in their fullness over Jonah, underneath him, all around him. So too, it seems, the psalmist. And again, when I come across these resonances, I'm inclined to hear them as mere coincidence. Still today, when people are burdened, they speak in drowning metaphors.

Theologian Stanley Hauerwas grew up the son of a mason, and in his memoir, Hauerwas quotes a passage from another memoir, one by a bricklayer:

> With hammer, mallet and chisel we have shaped and fashioned rough boulders. We often curse our material, and often we speak to it kindly—we have to come to terms with it in order to master it, and it has a way of dictating to us sometimes—and then the struggle begins. We try to impose ourselves on it, but we know our material and respect it. We will often take a suggestion from it, and our work will be the better for it.

Hauerwas reads this passage as speaking not only to the work of masons like his father, but also the work of theologians like himself, as both are a "craft requiring years of training." The mason learns to respect his material, to take suggestions from it, to struggle against it while figuring out how to make it do what he needs it to do. The mason must "come to terms" with it—must find the language, the *terms*, to do the work that needs to be done, and in finding those terms, learn to work both with them and against them.

Learning to lay bricks is an apprenticeship and, for Hauerwas, so is learning to write theology. Just as a mason must come to terms with rocks and boulders, "Theologians," Hauerwas writes, "do not get to choose the words they use." I do not think Hauerwas is speaking to, or of, theologians alone. Whenever a writer enters a field of inquiry —whether theology or, for me, whales—the writer does not get to choose her words. They are given her, and the writer must learn how to turn them her own way. Hauerwas continues:

> Because they do not get to choose the words they use they are forced to think hard about why the words they use are the ones that must be used. They must also do the equally hard work of thinking about the order that the words they use must have if the words are to do the work they are meant to do.

This process of thinking hard about what words must be used and in what order so that they are able to do the work they are meant to do is all-consuming. It demands immersing the self within a subject, a discipline, a discourse, a language, within particular ways of reading and writing, particular ways of listening and speaking. Poet Heather Christle describes it like this:

> Writing a poem is not so very different from digging a hole. It is work. You try to learn what you can from other holes and the people who dug before you. The difficulty comes from people who do not dig or spend time in holes thinking that the holes ought not be so wet, or dark, or full of worms. "Why is your hole not lined with light?" Sir, it is a hole.

Christle's dismissive of people who've not yet spent time in holes. But those kinds of questions—questions based off observations of the materials handed down—are the ones every apprentice must learn to ask, whether digging holes, writing poems, or learning to pray.

Jean Giono and his friend Lucien Jacques translated *Moby-Dick* into French—it took three years—"But long before I embarked on this project," Giono writes, "for at least five or six years, Melville's book was my foreign companion." What does it mean for a book to be your foreign companion for nearly a decade, to accompany you wherever you go, for Melville to be at your side years on end, his words inflecting yours, his presence a shadow alongside yours, his concerns yours, and yours his? Here's Giono again, describing how, through reading, he came to know (and be) Ishmael:

> When I was left alone in the dark, I had a clearer understanding of the soul of that patrician hero who takes command of *Moby-Dick*. He would accompany me on my homeward path. I never had to take more than a few steps to catch up with him and, once the depths of the shadows were black, to become him. I would reach him with what felt like a single, longer stride. Then it was as though I'd entered inside his skin, my body clothed in his like an overcoat.

Giono has entered into the text, putting it on like a second skin, his own ways of being thoroughly enveloped within the words of another. It's not unlike how Christle describes reading another poet: "I wrapped Plath's paragraphs over myself like a winding sheet."

So too has Ishmael entered into a text. After measuring a sperm whale skeleton, he tattoos its dimensions on his right arm, since "there was no other secure way of preserving such valuable statistics." Clothed in a sleeve of cetology, Ishmael becomes a Jonah here, his arm inside this whale. He doesn't include "the odd inches" when tattooing the measurements on his arm for he "wished the other parts of my body to remain a blank page for a poem I was then composing," a poem that will take up "what untattooed parts might remain."

I like to think that poem is *Moby-Dick*, and I picture Ishmael's body—his arm covered in numbers, his chest, back, and thighs covered in words. Whereas Giono wears Ishmael's words like a jacket, Ishmael inscribes words onto his very self. He is inside those sentences, his body wrapped in letters, the whale athwart him. Reading his words suddenly becomes quite intimate, Ishmael inviting me to pore over, to scrutinize, to hold in my hands, to run my fingers over his text, over his body, over these words made flesh, his own body attesting how wide and long and high and deep is the whale.

Reciting Jonah daily, I begin to wonder what it means to recite a passage and what it means to *pray* it. I do not think, as I churn through the verses, that I am praying them. I'm not sure who my audience is. Praying, it seems, should involve some sort of intention as to how the words are put together. Some sort of authorship. I find myself with the skepticism Kathleen Norris, in this chapter's epigraph, describes, a suspicion of words handed over to me. This preference for originality, this distrust of a script, comes, I think, from the individualism and exceptionalism I, as an American, am awash in. And, I admit, I find it easier to be within my own bland and comfortable words than to find myself within—inhabit, even—the words of another, especially when praying.

But then I remember monastics who, through years of practice, memorize the entire Psalter and, along the way, train themselves to continually pray, with each inhale and exhale from their lungs, "Lord Jesus Christ, Son of God, have mercy on me, a sinner," the very act of breathing transfigured into prayer. These sisters and brothers are not composing new prayers, they are not speaking extemporaneously, they make no claims to originality. They're saying words given them, words millennia old, words infused into their respiration. They find something redemptive in those inherited words, a freedom in using a script.

Might Jonah be doing the same? Reciting his prayers, working a script inside the belly of the whale? The similarities are just too numerous, the next verse in Jonah's prayer aligning with Psalm 31 and Psalm 5:

Then I said, "I am driven away from your sight; Yet I shall again look upon your holy temple.	I had said in my alarm, "I am cut off from your sight." But I, through the abundance of your steadfast love, will enter your house.

Here, too, the resonance between Jonah and the Psalms seems like it could be due to somewhat generic circumstances—a prophet driven away from God yearning to return. It's a narrative of redemption, commonplace enough. But as Jonah's prayer continues, *resonance* seems too weak a word for what I'm hearing between Jonah and the Psalms. So too, *echo* doesn't seem strong enough to describe what's happening. The next two verses, set alongside passages from Psalms 69 and 116:

The waters closed in over me to take
my life;
  the deep surrounded me;
Weeds were wrapped around my head
  at the roots of the mountains.
I went down to the land
  whose bars closed upon me forever;

I sink in the deep mire,
  where there is no foothold;
I have come into deep waters,
  and the flood sweeps over me.
The snares of death encompassed
me;
  the pangs of Sheol laid hold on me;

Jonah, weeds wrapped around his legs, sinking down to the roots of the mountains, barred in by the land itself—such images, such poetry. Alongside it, the psalmist writes of death having snares, of its very pangs laying hold of the poet, dragging the poet into the pit. It's a sinking image, both poet and prophet in a straitjacket, one of seaweed, the other death itself.

The psalmist's *I* is one I could inhabit myself, "The flood sweeps over me" vague enough that it invites me into its syntax. I could make a home there, inside those words, and a few years ago, I did. When hospitalized for what was thought to be cancer, I said, alongside the psalmist, that the snares of death had encompassed me. That verse became my own.

Injecting myself into those words, I realize I am doing the same as Jonah. He, too, inhabits the Psalms. The *I* of his prayer is at once his and yet also an *I* he shares with the psalmist, with fellow Israelites, and with others in distress. Like mine, his *I* is communal. It's a plural *I* inflected by the words of others, both of us, together, inhabiting the language of another—the psalmist—relying on that inherited language to name our own experience, to speak through us.

Melville knew himself as a writer, his processes and his proclivities. As one scholar puts it, Melville knew he was "a writer who borrowed heavily from previous writers," such that *Moby-Dick* "would itself be the original product of the assimilation of many other books." *Moby-Dick*, then, isn't a book only about whales. It's a book about reading, about writing, about a writer and his sources, about a writer learning to use the words those sources offer. It's about inheriting certain ways of being in relation to a subject at hand and locating the self within them.

And this is how I read the Extracts: I imagine Melville, his desk covered in clippings sent him by friends, books open and others dog-eared, composing as my dissertation adviser recommended. I imagine him trying to learn how to use a word by observing its use, recording it, then experimenting with how else it might be used. "Usufruct" is how Charles Olson describes this writing method. Melville enters into the whale himself, spending time inside these words, learning how to live with them, learning, too, what they mean when placed next to others. In the Extracts, *great* appears fourteen times, variations of *monster* eight times, *mouth* five times, variations of *jaw* six times. Laden with biblical weight, *leviathan* appears eleven times, modified by *great, that sea beast, huge, dread, that piercing serpent*, and *that crooked serpent*. As Melville gathers his extracts, he learns the nuances these words carry. His is a rich inheritance.

When I review the letters Melville wrote while composing *Moby-Dick*, I read a Melville somewhat scared of his manuscript. Uneasy with it. Not sure what to do with it, a bit repulsed but attracted to it nonetheless. He's written something grotesque yet sublime. In one of these letters, he warns a friend not to buy *Moby-Dick*: "It is by no means the sort of book for you." (I'm not sure it's the sort of book for me, either: I first read it in 2005, but it would be another twelve years before I'd successfully reread *Moby-Dick*, with eight failed attempts in the interim, each time quitting a hundred pages in.)

In another letter, Melville calls *Moby-Dick* "a wicked book," but he glories in it, referring to the manuscript as "my 'Whale'" (I hear, here, Thoreau's "my beans"), and he makes an offer:

> Shall I send you a fin of the *Whale* by way of a specimen mouthful? The tail is not yet cooked—though the hell-fire in which the whole book is broiled might not unreasonably have cooked it all ere this.

It would be easy to read Melville here as melodramatic—for Melville, the book *is* a whale—but consider the following, a passage in *Moby-Dick* wherein Ishmael describes trying to write the whale. I cannot help but read this passage as Melville justifying his style:

> Applied to any other creature than the Leviathan—to an ant or a flea— such portly terms might justly be deemed unwarrantably grandilo- quent. But when Leviathan is the text, the case is altered. Fain am I to stagger to this emprise under the weightiest words of the dictionary.

Ishmael says the dictionary is giving him its weightiest words, but so too is tradition—the whaling industry, scripture, literature, and science writing. I take Ishmael as a stand-in for Melville in this moment, and Melville doesn't get to choose the words he uses. And he knows, too, that to wield these words he needs more than just any old writing instrument. "Give me a condor's quill! Give me Vesuvius' crater for an inkstand!" He—Ishmael? Melville?—calls for his arms to be held up as he becomes faint from the writing. It's exhausting. "To produce a mighty book," he proclaims, "you must choose a mighty theme." So too, it seems, you must have mighty tools and mighty words—and a little help from your friends.

Writing about whales, then, necessitates a certain kind of book, a certain methodology. I see this in the many whale books on my shelf. A lot of them are unconventional, and delightfully so. I've been given most, the others I've searched out at used bookstores. (I go straight to the Nature section; often, in coastal towns, within it I find a shelf devoted to Whales.) There's Matt Kish's *Moby-Dick in Pictures*, Kish drawing one image for each of his Signet edition's 552 pages. There's *A Whaler's Dictionary*, Dan Beachy-Quick writing prose poem definitions for key words in *Moby-Dick*, words like Jonah, Whiteness, Whale (Ghost), and Etymology. Each entry ends with a list of cross-references: Coffin is cross-referenced with Death, Dictionary, Experience, Faith, Friendship, Hieroglyph, Reading (Epistemology), Savage, Spermaceti, Starry Archipelagoes, Tablet, Tattoo, and Truth. Beachy-Quick advises against reading the book straight through; read it like a dictionary, he says, jumping from entry to entry as inquiry demands. (I'm disobedient; I read it cover to cover. Twice.)

There's *The Whale Building Book: A Step by Step Guide to Preparing and Assembling Medium-Sized Whale Skeletons* and *The Sperm Whale Engineering Manual, or, Building a Big Whale Skeleton, with a Gray Whale Skeleton Project Addendum*, both self-published by Lee Post—people call him the Bone Man—books full of hundreds of Post's meticulous (or perhaps obsessive, in an Ahabian sense) sketches of each and every whale bone from multiple angles coupled with equally meticulous directions for how to put those bones together. In a stack of maritime-themed comics (a curious genre eventually eclipsed by superheroes), I found a 1966 comic book titled, in bold red letters, *MOBY DICK*, its cover showing the white whale fighting two plesiosaurs. It's in Spanish, and from the pictures and some poor attempts at translation, I read a story about a shirtless giant wrestling a *Tyrannosaurus rex* and failing until Moby Dick comes to his aid. I've also got a novel about Captain Ahab's wife (I'm tempted to call it fan fiction, but not at all in a derogatory way; it's quite good in how it builds on Melville's work) and a *Moby-Dick* children's book using only twelve words to tell the story.

These are just a handful. I've dozens more, and I've come to think the books in my whale library are unconventional because the figure in whose wake they write was himself pushed toward the unconventional. After all, Ishmael does claim, "There are some enterprises in which a careful disorderliness is the true method." I want to read that line as self-referential, Melville commenting, knowingly, on how unconventional his own book is. These writers work within a tradition Melville himself worked within, his influence looming even when he's not cited. *Melville* has become a word we whale writers do not get to choose.

Bartholomae tells a story about learning to use words—not unlike when my students and I were learning to say *whale*. He's in graduate school, studying under Richard Poirier. Bartholomae is taken with

Poirier. He wants "to be able to read and speak and write like him." And so, Bartholomae practices:

> I would, for example, copy out difficult or impressive sentences he had written in order to get the feel of them. I can feel them now in the many sentences I write. It is a mixed feeling. I state it simply, but it was not simple at all.

It is not simple because this is imitation couched within tradition. It is a writer trying to use words and learning, too, to ask them to do certain kinds of work, and through this learning, find himself within the words.

> I tried for a whole semester to write a paper using the word "language" as he used it in talking about how language "worked" in "Upon Appleton House." It took me a whole semester to use the word in a sentence that actually made sense to me.

I wish Bartholomae had included some of the sentences he wrote that did not make sense to him. A whole semester to learn to use a noun and how to pair it with its verb is a long time. Then again, monastics spend a lifetime learning to pray a psalm, learning how to use these words, learning what they mean when paired with other words not chosen but inherited.

I wonder, too, how Bartholomae would say "language" behaves when paired with "worked"—that is, what this noun and verb do together that other combinations cannot. Bartholomae was testing how to use these words, words couched within history, expectation, desire, and convention, and learning, through his writing, how to be present on the page within those inherited words. Such presence comes when he begins working within and against the words. Bartholomae explains:

> And in my own writing, I'll confess, I have taken titles from Poirier's essays as my own—or, knowingly or unknowingly, I recall or cite (or I channel or appropriate) his sentences and paragraphs and put them to use on a subject . . . that he did not or could not or would not reference.

Bartholomae comes to be a writer himself only once he has imitated, appropriated, and found himself within sentences. It's a self-definition through relationship, the self entirely dependent on the work of others. Note, too, that Bartholomae puts Poirier's sentences "to use on a subject" that was beyond Poirier's own concerns. "This way of reading does violence to his prose," Bartholomae admits, "Still, this is how I read the work, completing his sentences by turning them my way." Bartholomae inherits words from Poirier, who himself inherited them from his teachers, and so on, and so on, and so on. He learns how to use those words, learns what work they can be made to do, and then puts them to work on a project of his own.

The prayer turns, and this turn, too, has a companion in the Psalms, this time Psalm 30:

Yet you brought up my life from the pit, O Lord my God.

O Lord, you have brought up my soul from Sheol;
you restored me to life from among those
who go down to the pit.

There is not a single line in Jonah's prayer he could call his own, not a single line that does not find itself in the Psalms. I am unsure the verb that would best articulate what Jonah does. Does he *pilfer* from the Psalms? *Pull* from them? *Borrow*? *Plagiarize*? Those verbs suggest some sort of ill-character. They carry within them a critique of a writer's seeming inability to be original. To say Jonah *steals* from the Psalms is to expect a writer to say something that's never been said before, and to believe it's a fault to do otherwise. Nor is he just *quoting* them. Jonah's use of the Psalms runs much deeper than mere quotation.

I'm inclined to say Jonah has *appropriated* these Psalms, *internalized* them, even, such that their words have become his own. Jonah draws from the past to speak to his present. He's not just quoting these Psalms; he's arranging their sentences into something new, something entirely his own even as it is taken from others. He is composing, as Bartholomae was with Poirier, turning these sentences his own way, putting them to use on a subject—being stuck in the belly of a whale—the psalmist likely could not imagine.

Near the end of the prayer, Jonah recounts teetering on the edge of death, and he appropriates Psalms 142, 77, and 18:

When my life was fainting away,	When my spirit faints within me,
I remembered the Lord,	I will remember the deeds of the Lord.
and my prayer came to you,	From his temple he heard my voice,
into your holy temple.	and my cry to him reached his ears.

I don't want to suggest that Jonah is some pawn—that, as a prophet, he's just a mouthpiece with no ability to speak his own sentences. Nor do I want to suggest he's falling back on pat, comfortable, commonplace language. Even though his sentences are shared with others, they are not cliché. The words he speaks are of his being, of his own tongue, even as they are from another, such that, when he needs sentences, those sentences come forth from his inherited language. The Psalms provide him words when he has none. I might even say he finds himself, there, in the belly of the whale, at a point of vibrant intersection with the Psalms.

These, the final verses of Jonah's prayer, set alongside verses again appropriated from the Psalms (in this case, Psalms 31, 50, and 3):

Those who pay regard to vain idols	I hate those who pay regard to
forsake their hope of steadfast love.	worthless idols, but I trust in the Lord.
But I with the voice of thanksgiving	Offer to God a sacrifice of
will sacrifice to you;	thanksgiving,
What I have vowed I will pay	Perform your vows to the Most High.
Salvation belongs to the Lord!	Salvation belongs to the Lord.

When I recite Jonah's prayer, I hear someone who has learned how to use the words he's been given. I hear a prophet steeped in a discourse, steeped in a community, steeped in a shared language, such that that language, community, and discourse shape what he says.

There's a certain beauty here. This reluctant prophet, this prophet on the run, this prophet who goes to great lengths to avoid prophesying—when he speaks, he speaks not his own words but words inherited. He prophesies.

In his memoir about traveling to monasteries on Mount Athos, poet Scott Cairns tells of sitting alongside a monk whose "conversation was woven with the writings of the Fathers, whose words he had long since internalized, and made his own." Cairns seeks to do the same, to splice these ancient words into his own sentences, the rhythms of his own speech inflected by tradition. With the monks, Cairns has "an experience of words I had read, but had not yet owned, had not yet performed, had not yet made flesh." He knows the words he has been given. He does not yet know how to use them, how to be present within them, how to turn these words into his own flesh, his own being.

That's the question, isn't it, how to inhabit inherited words? I am not sure I know what it means to recite Jonah's prayer, or what it means to—or how I might—pray it, or how I might inhabit Jonah's *I*, or how my son, having received part of Jonah's prayer from us, his parents, might inherit these words and, maybe someday, inhabit them. But I spend time inside these sentences, inside these ancient phrases translated from another language—another experience—to my own, inside these words handed down. I read them, I reread them, I speak them, I hear them. I hoist myself up on them, move about and within them. For if I can learn to inhabit these inherited sentences, dwell inside these words I do not get to choose, maybe even incarnate them somehow—perhaps then I might learn to bide my time within the belly of the whale.

INTERLUDE } Extracts

The Extracts opening *Moby-Dick*—seventy-nine of them spread over nine pages—are gathered, Ishmael says, by a "sub-sub-librarian." He's a "mere painstaking burrower and grub worm of a poor devil" who has scrounged around in search of any and every passage he can find about whales. He's searched high and low, "through the long Vaticans and street-stalls of the earth." And he has not been discriminating in what he collects, "picking up whatever random allusions to whales he could anyways find in any book whatsoever, sacred or profane."

When I read of this sub-sub-librarian's scavenger reading practice, I think of another compiler, Virginia Tufte, she of sentences. She published two books about them—*Grammar as Style* in 1971 and *Artful Sentences* in 2006—and they are quite similar: Tufte culls a sentence from her reading, and presents it with short commentary on what a reader might notice about how that sentence moves on the page. She then offers another sentence, with a bit more commentary, and so on, each book collecting hundreds upon hundreds of sentences sitting alongside Tufte's commentaries in an effort to teach how someone might read a sentence and how someone might write one too.

Ishmael is trying to know whales; Tufte, sentences, and her method is not unlike his. Both scour. "The search was made," Tufte writes, "through reviews, quarterlies, and journals, learned and otherwise; through all sorts of popular magazines, newspapers, and collected journalism; through biography, history, studies in social and political science, art, and literature; and through original literature itself, essays, stories, and novels." She takes her sentences "from any place good writing is going on."

But Tufte hesitates to lay down firm prescriptions about what makes a good sentence. The breadth of her collection prohibits it. She explains:

> Although I have examined a fair number of samples—many more than are quoted—it may well be that in some instances other samples would have supported different conclusions. I hesitate even to use the word *conclusions*; *observations* is more accurate. The book is exploratory rather than definitive, and its *method* is more important than its statements.

Its method *is more important than its statements.* Ishmael says the same. Of the Extracts, he warns, "Therefore you must not, in every case at least, take the higgledy-piggledy whale statements, however authentic, in these extracts, for veritable gospel cetology." The Extracts can give "a glancing bird's eye view" he says, not of the whale itself but "of what has been promiscuously said, thought, fancied, and sung of Leviathan." Melville, Ishmael, and their sub-sub-librarian are not trying to give an authoritative account of the whale—to do so would be impossible—but to show how people have tried to write the whale. The method is more important than the statements.

I want to read the Extracts as a commonplace book of sorts, Melville copying down passages about whales, gathering them together, presenting them without commentary through the narrative device of Ishmael and his sub-sub-librarian, the method here an argument itself about how someone might come to know, about how someone might locate the self amid and against these whales, these texts. It's an effort, again, to find a place where language might yield some point of vibrant intersection.

I, too, keep a commonplace book. It's a black notebook, and in it I gather passages compelling and provocative, passages whose sentences I admire, passages I imagine I could use in my writing or my teaching. And for the past ten years, I've also been gathering retellings of Jonah's story, those I find too compelling and provocative to ignore, the practice of curating them another attempt at knowing.

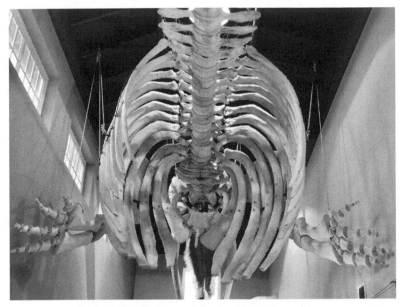

The view inside the belly of a thirty-eight-foot gray whale.

And the Lord appointed a great fish to swallow up Jonah.

—The Book of Jonah

Have a care how you seize the privilege of Jonah alone; the privilege
of discoursing upon the joists and beams; the rafters, ridge-pole,
sleepers, and underpinnings, making up the frame-work of the
leviathan; and belike of the tallow-vats, dairy-rooms, butteries, and
cheeseries in his bowels.

—Ishmael
Moby-Dick

Now listen right good while I tell you this tale
How Jonah the prophet got caught by this whale
That whale caught poor Jonah and bless your dear soul
It not only caught him, it swallowed him whole

—The New Lost City Ramblers
"The Old Fish Song"

For just as Jonah was three days and three nights in the belly of the
great fish, so will the Son of Man be three days and three nights in
the heart of the earth.

—Jesus
The Gospel of Saint Matthew

Jarvis, you ever hear the tale of Jonah?

—Ironman,
Marvel's *The Avengers*

I knew a whale in California who said it was a descendant of the
great fish God prepared for Jonah.

—Diane Glancy
"The Lord Spoke to the Fish"

Imagine the silence Jonah heard, in the mouth of the whale deep in
the ocean.

—Dan Beachy-Quick
A Whaler's Dictionary

The bones of sailors from the north
And sailors from the east
Lay high in a pyre
In the belly of a beast
A beast should you wander in its path
Upon your ship and your flesh he'll sup
You'll disappear from this world
Until you've been swallowed up

—Bruce Springsteen
"Swallowed Up (In the Belly of the Whale)"

When I moved back in with my mom, the door to my old room,
to my old life in that room, it opened up like a mouth and
swallowed me.

—Edwin Black,
Tommy Orange's *There There*

The coroner's report suggests that Evelyn died inside the whale's stomach. Meaning she was *eaten alive.*

—Batman
Detective Comics

A wild rolling whale, as fate would have it,
Flung up from the abyss, was floating by that boat
And was aware of that man as the water reached for him,
And rushed to swallow him, opening his maw.

—The Pearl Poet
"Patience"

But at that very moment the monster stuck his head out of the water, opened his huge mouth, and swallowed the canoe, with Kwatee's brother in it.

—Kwatee and the Lake Monster

Then, up from those sunless depths, or yet also down from foam-starred heavens, a totem-red, tartan-green impossibility descended or arose, its body so massive and shining, visage so travel-scarred and ancient, that I was swallowed like Jonah by the sight. I know no better way to invoke the being's presence than to state the naked name: *Coho.*

—David James Duncan
My Story as Told by Water:
Confessions, Druidic Rants, Reflections, Bird-Watchings,
Fish-Stalkings, Visions, Songs and Prayers Refracting Light,
from Living Rivers, in the Age of the Industrial Dark

A great big enormous trout came up—ker-pflop-p-p-p! with a splash—and it seized Mr. Jeremy with a snap, "Ow! Ow! Ow!"—and then it turned and dived down to the bottom of the pond!

But the trout was so displeased with the taste of the macintosh, that in less than half a minute it spat him out again.

—Beatrix Potter
The Tale of Mr. Jeremy Fisher

I once more dived within the skeleton.

—Ishmael
Moby-Dick

To enter this gigantic body alive is equivalent to descending into
Hell, to confronting the ordeals destined for the dead.

—Mircea Eliade
Rites and Symbols of Initiation

He has swallowed me like a monster.

—The Book of Jeremiah

One of the lads on another ship had the misfortune, in full view of
his comrades, to become isolated from the others on an ice pan,
from which he fell into the icy waters in the proximity of a huge
sperm whale. . . . Somehow the poor fellow was swallowed by the
whale.

—Egerton Y. Davis Jr.
"Man in Whale"

Over this lip, as over a slippery threshold, we now slide into the
mouth. . . . Good Lord! is this the road that Jonah went?

—Ishmael
Moby-Dick

The next moment it got dark and I felt some pressure on my hip,
and once I felt the pressure I instantly knew a whale had grabbed
me. I could not imagine in my head how he was actually holding
me or grabbing me but I could feel the pressure on my hip. . . . I
became the inside man.

—Rainer Schimpf,
after being taken into the mouth of a Bryde's Whale

MARLIN: We're in a whale. Don't you get it?

DORY: A whale?

MARLIN: A whale. 'Cause you had to ask for help. And now we're stuck here.

—Walt Disney's *Finding Nemo*

I shall not go into detail on the great size of sea monsters as described by those who know, but the skeleton which had upheld the body of such a one was displayed in public for the people at Carthage, and everyone knows how many men could be enclosed in that space. What an immense opening that mouth had, like the gateway of a cave!

—Saint Augustine
Letter 102, written to Deogratias

With a lantern we might descend into the great Kentucky Mammoth Cave of his stomach.

—Ishmael
Moby-Dick

Are there some things He wants us to learn that we can't learn except by falling into the abyss? Is that why the Jonah of old, who could not say "thy will be done," had to lie three days and three nights in the dark in the belly of the great fish?

—Jayber,
in Wendell Berry's *Jayber Crow*

But for me, the vow of stability has been the belly of the whale.

—Thomas Merton
The Sign of Jonas

Sitting upright and riding in the cab of the truck, his muscles began to jerk, his arms flailed, his mouth opened to make way for cries that would not come. His pale face twitched and grimaced. He might have been Jonah clinging wildly to the whale's tongue.

—Flannery O'Connor
The Violent Bear It Away

The sperm whale has no tongue. It swallowed a prophet to speak.

—Dan Beachy-Quick
The Whaler's Dictionary

No other human word is so thoroughly inhabited by another
species than the word *whale*.

—Aaron Moe
Protean Poetics

But the whale rushed round in a sudden maelstrom; seized the
swimmer between his jaws; and rearing high up with him, plunged
headlong again, and went down.

—Ishmael
Moby-Dick

JIMINY CRICKET: Hey! It's a message!
PINOCCHIO: What's it say?
JIMINY CRICKET: It's about your father.
PINOCCHIO: Where is he?
JIMINY CRICKET: Why, uh, uh, it says here he, uh, he went looking for you,
    and uh, uh, was swallowed by a whale.
PINOCCHIO: Swallowed by a whale?
JIMINY CRICKET: Yeah, uh-huh, a whale! A whale named Monstro! But, but
    wait! He's alive!
PINOCCHIO: Alive! Where?
JIMINY CRICKET: Why, uh, uh, inside the whale at the, at the bottom of
    the sea.

—Walt Disney's *Pinocchio*

My God! poor Tashtego . . . dropped head-foremost down into this
great Tun of Heidelberg, and with a horrible oily gurgling, went
clean out of sight!

—Ishmael
Moby-Dick

He had found himself engulfed and sliding down a slippery
channel, the walls of which quivered at his touch.

—William Kastner
"Man in Whale"

It was in Queen Anne's time that the bone was in its glory, the
farthingale being then all the fashion. . . . Those ancient dames
moved about gaily, though in the jaws of the whale, as you may say;
even so, in a shower, with the like thoughtlessness, do we nowadays
fly under the same jaws for protection; the umbrella being a tent
spread over the same bone.

—Ishmael
Moby-Dick

How heel over head was I hurled down
the broad road of its throat, stopped inside
its chest wide as a hall, and like Jonas I stood up

—Lynn Emanuel
"My Life"

Joseph cannot believe the size of it; maybe this whale had a large
heart or maybe all whales have hearts this big, but the heart is the
size of a riding mower. The tubes running into it are large enough
to stick his head into.

—Anthony Doerr
"The Caretaker"

Imagine, for the largest of whales, a heart the size of a farm tractor
tire. Your whole body could fit inside one of these organs.

—Nick Pyenson
Spying on Whales

Its heart is so large a grown man can curl into one chamber
and sleep.

—Dan Beachy-Quick
A Whaler's Dictionary

The biggest heart in the world is inside the blue whale. It weighs
more than seven tons. It's as big as a room. It *is* a room, with four
chambers. A child could walk around in it, head high, bending only
to step through the valves. The valves are as big as the swinging
doors in a saloon.

—Brian Doyle
"Joyas Voladoras"

But come out now, and look at this portentous lower jaw, which
seems like the long narrow lid of an immense snuff-box, with the
hinge at one end, instead of one side. If you pry it up, so as to get it
overhead, and expose its rows of teeth, it seems a terrific portcullis.

—Ishmael
Moby-Dick

Two or three times on my visit I sat under the blue whale's jaw,
or even within the cage of its chest, the thick portcullis of its ribs
descending around.

—Kathleen Jamie
Sightlines

In his amazing bulk, portcullis jaw, and omnipotent tail, there was
enough to appal the stoutest man.

—Ishmael
Moby-Dick

For the fact is that being inside a whale is a very comfortable, cosy,
homelike thought.

—George Orwell
"Inside the Whale"

The whale's towering rib cage had become a cathedral for worms,
snails, and crabs, which grazed beneath its buttresses.

—Jeffrey Marlow
"A Whale's Afterlife"

It finally dawned upon him that he had been swallowed by the
whale, and he was overcome by horror at the situation. . . .
He knew there was no hope of escape from his strange prison.
He tried to look at it bravely, but the terrible quiet, darkness and
heat, combined with the horrible knowledge of his environment,
overcame him.

—Sir Francis Fox
Sixty-Three Years of Engineering, Scientific and Social Work

For truly, the Right Whale's mouth would accommodate a couple
of whist-tables, and comfortably seat all the players.

—Ishmael
Moby-Dick

Upon news of a whale being taken, they are rowed over to the
works on a boat. The whalers dig a sort of narrow grave in the
body, and in this the patient lies for two hours, as in a Turkish
bath, the decomposing blubber of the whale closing around his
body and acting as a huge poultice. The whalers make no charge
for a dip in the whale, and go on with their work on another part
of the body while the patient is enjoying his immersion.

—"A New Cure for Rheumatism"
New York Times, 7 March 1896

In 1827 a blue whale taken off Ostend was reduced to its skeleton
and toured from Ghent to Brussels, Rotterdam and Berlin before
arriving, four years later, in London. . . . Customers could quaff
wine while sitting in the animal's ribcage, an "unwonted saloon."
They were, however, not treated to the twenty-four-piece orchestra
that performed within the whale during its European sojourn.

—Philip Hoare
The Whale

Projecting from the further angle of the room stands a dark-
looking den—the bar—a rude attempt at a right whale's head. Be
that how it may, there stands the vast arched bone of the whale's
jaw, so wide, a coach might almost drive beneath it. Within are
shabby shelves, ranged round with old decanters, bottles, flasks;
and in those jaws of swift destruction, like another cursed Jonah
(by which name indeed they called him), bustles a little withered
old man, who, for their money, dearly sells the sailors deliriums
and death.

—Ishmael
Moby-Dick

Oh this has been such a Jonah day, Marilla. I'm so ashamed of
myself.

—Anne
Anne of Avonlea

Jonah, Ezekiel, Daniel, he was at that moment all of them—the
swallowed, the lowered, the enclosed.

—Flannery O'Connor
The Violent Bear It Away

Look down, we befeech thee, and hear us, calling out of the depth
of mifery, and out of the jaws of this death, which is ready now to
fwallow us up: Save, Lord, or elfe we perifh.

—The Book of Common Prayer and Administration of the Sacraments
and other Rites and Ceremonies of the Church,
according to the Ufe of the Church of England:
together with the Psalter of Psalms of David,
Pointed as they are to be fung or faid in Churches

Was the great fish like the dog with a favorite toy in its mouth that
won't let go no matter how hard you shake its head back and forth?

—Diane Glancy
"The Lord Spoke to the Fish"

He had come from the belly of the beast.

—Stanley Hauerwas
Hannah's Child: A Theologian's Memoir

Presently, Q'wäetí is forced to sink by the man-eater. Q'wäetí is
swallowed, gets inside the belly of the whale, seizes his knife, takes
it and cuts back and forth through the whale's intestines.

—Q'wäetí and the Man-Eating Whale

The whale was killed and in a few hours was lying by the ship's
side and the crew were busy with axes and spades removing the
blubber. . . . The sailors were startled by something in it which gave
spasmodic signs of life, and inside was found the missing sailor
doubled up and unconscious.

—Sir Francis Fox
Sixty-Three Years of Engineering, Scientific and Social Work

After manacling his hands and feet, the committee drew the chains
taut, passed them around the creature's back, and locked them.
Concealed by screens while the orchestra entertained, Houdini
came forth from the belly of the acrid corpse in fifteen minutes,
greasy but grinning.

—Kenneth Silverman
Houdini!!! The Career of Ehrich Weiss:
American Self-Liberator, Europe's Eclipsing Sensation,
World's Handcuff King & Prison Breaker

Within the body of the monster, within the belly of Leviathan, lurks
the intestinal labyrinth whose amazed complexity unfolds into the
secrets by which the universe itself formed.

—Dan Beachy-Quick
A Whaler's Dictionary

And the Lord spoke to the fish, and it vomited Jonah out upon the
dry land.

—The Book of Jonah

FIVE } Within

And Jonah was in the belly of the fish three days and three nights.
—Jonah 1.17

"You could always get a sperm donor." The doctor points to a sheet of paper. "You see, this column shows the normal range, and this is where you tested." We'd been trying to conceive for a year. "You have less than 1 percent of the average man, and what you have isn't swimming at all. But there are options. Like I said, you could get a donor." We leave the office, sit in the car, and cry.

In April 1947, *Natural History* published a letter from William Kastner, of St. Louis, Missouri, seeking clarification from an expert concerning "an apparently sincere account of a man who was swallowed by a whale in February 1891 and lived to tell the tale." Kastner had read the story "in one of the popular magazines." The letter echoes, unintentionally, the one Deogratias sent Saint Augustine, in 409, asking whether Jonah's story is true.

The man Kastner wonders about is James Bartley. He was allegedly sailing on the *Star of the East* whaleship in the Falkland Islands. The ship lowered its skiffs for a chase, a whale stove one, and Bartley was knocked overboard. The crew assumed he drowned. They proceeded to kill the whale, pull alongside it, and begin the long hours of flensing. While continuing their work the next morning, the crew noticed something inside the whale's belly. They cut it open and found Bartley, "doubled up inside, unconscious." There are three things

Kastner thinks may have accounted for Bartley's supposed survival, and these are what he seeks comment on: "(1) The whale's 'serrated teeth' had missed his body, (2) the man had lost consciousness and remained quiet, and (3) the whale had soon been killed, which lowered its body temperature."

Kastner receives a response from Dr. Robert Cushman Murphy, who *Natural History* tells readers "has gone out with the whalers from New Bedford, as well as with the Norwegian whalers in Antarctic waters, and is one of the few scientists to have studied the old-time Yankee whaling methods firsthand." *Natural History* wants readers to know Murphy is an authority: he's not only educated, he's been on the water too. Murphy doesn't respond to Kastner's three queries directly, but he does note it's possible a man could be swallowed by a whale. Whales swallow other big things, he writes, like seals. (Years earlier, in 1927, the Reverend Ambrose John Wilson, at pains to prove Jonah's story, argued, in the *Princeton Theological Review*, that it must have been a sperm whale that swallowed Jonah, since sperm whales do not chew their prey but swallow it whole and have a throat large enough to swallow a human.) Murphy then claims that inside the belly a man would live only as long as he could hold his breath. This tale has all the trappings of "cliché," Murphy writes, and he concludes "I am constrained to say that the story is unadulterated 'bunk.'"

Constrained to say. What a curious phrase. I read in it a desire, on the part of Murphy, that the story be true, a desire in tension with the much stronger language of "unadulterated 'bunk.'" He is constrained to say, obligated even. Does he say it's *bunk* unwillingly then? Or, at least, is he disappointed to say it? And, in even asking about Bartley, Kastner seems, at least as I read him, to have a sense of wonder, a sense of possibility, a hope, perhaps, that the story be true. I read Kastner and Murphy as reaching for something.

Even more curious, then, how Murphy concludes his response. As he argues Bartley's story is not true, and though he suspects "the *Star of the East* may well be wholly apocryphal," Murphy finishes with this, these his final words on the matter: "I would not categorically assert that." He leaves the door open, barely.

When Sir Francis Fox retells Bartley's story (toward the end of a book about railways, tunnels, and building restoration, a strange place to talk about a man in a whale), he tries to convince readers, and perhaps himself, that it's true. He notes that he came across the story in two sources—"One evidently by the captain of the whaler; the other probably by one of his officers"—and "The incident was carefully investigated by two scientists—one of whom was the late M. de Parville, the senior editor of the *Journal des Débats* of Paris, well known as a man of sound judgment and a careful writer."

Note the many appeals to authority here: a captain, an officer, two scientists, one of them a careful writer. They're not unlike those in a 1771 account—from the exuberantly titled THE *Maſſachuſetts Gazette, AND Boſton* POST-BOY *and* THE ADVERTISER—recounting the story of one Marſhal Jenkins, pulled under by a whale only to then be thrown from it. (To retain the curiosities of eighteenth-century periodicals, I've retained the original typesetting.)

> We hear from Edgartown, that a Veſſel lately arrived there from a Whaling Voyage ; and that in her Voyage, one Marſhal Jenkins, with others, being in a Boat that ſtruck a Whale, ſhe turn'd and bit the Boat in two, took ſaid Jenkins in her Mouth, and went down with him ; but on her riſing threw him into one part, from whence he was taken on board the Veſſel by the Crew, being much bruis'd ; and that in about a Fortnight after, he perfectly recovered. This account we have from undoubted Authority.

There was apparently physical evidence of the encounter—people say the whale left permanent teeth marks on Jenkins—but the way it's written here, what's more important is where the reporter heard the story. The story is prefaced with "We hear from Edgartown" and closes with "This account we have from undoubted Authority." It's significant, too, that Jenkins's story is not front-page news for the *Gazette.* The headline that day is "*A Review of the preſent State of the* WAR *between the* Ruffians *and* Turks," which suggests that a man taken by a whale, a story relegated to the newspaper's third page, is not out of the ordinary. Its placement avoids sensationalizing the story by normalizing it, making the remarkable unremarkable. (The story following it announces, "the Rev. Mr. *Stevens* of Kittery is chofen to preach the next Dudlean Lecture at Harvard College.--The Subject, *Revealed Religion.*") As does Fox, as does *Natural History*, the *Gazette* wants me to trust them, trust their reporters, trust their sources, trust their story.

If I do, it seems I must trust Jonah too. And yet, I don't find this question whether Jonah could actually be within the whale and live to tell about it all that interesting. A few years ago, I heard a pastor offer nine proofs for Jonah's story, his sermon, to my mind, completely missing (perhaps willfully ignoring) mystery. The question I find more compelling: why is that belly so appealing?

Consider this: interviewing Ishmael, unsure whether he's fit for service on a whale boat, Captain Peleg asks a question that puts Ishmael in the belly of a whale: "Now, art thou the man to pitch a harpoon down a live whale's throat, and then jump after it? Answer, quick!" The question suggests a whaler would (and even should) voluntarily dive inside a whale. Just as Jonah is thrown overboard to save his shipmates, the captain seeks a whaler willing to throw himself down a whale's maw. For Captain Peleg, the impulse to dive down a whale's throat speaks to the courage necessary for whaling. But underneath that, I see something else: a yearning to be there, within.

To grieve the child we will not be able to have, to mourn dreams deferred, I begin fasting once a week, on Fridays. I want to hold our sorrow, to face it, to turn it around in my hands and come to know it, come to terms with it, find the language to begin to speak it.

Through my hunger I begin to see how most everything in my life comes on demand. I want a book so I buy it. I'm cold so I put on a sweater. I'm thirsty so I drink. A child, though, does not come on demand, and for us, may never at all. As I fast, there are three things

I learn, no, four, that stay with me: I learn to wait, learn to be patient, learn to stave off hunger, learn to forestall desire. When people ask, "When are you going to have kids?" my answer becomes "You can't really control that sort of thing," the fast showing me how many things are far, far outside my control.

A year into the fast, I receive a letter from my brother in Spokane, written on sheet music, his writing ignoring the staffs altogether. It's dated 17 March 2016. He announces he and my other brother are fasting on my and my wife's behalf, a two-day fast, beginning the sixteenth and ending the seventeenth, those days chosen for our birthdays. They're going to do this each month. "Prayer is such a mystery to me," he writes, "I don't expect to change God's mind." There's a sense, in that line, of the futility of a prayer, the futility of a fast. But they try anyway. "I do expect that we will feel your pain in a new way all through the day." He gives some caution, unaware of my own fast: "We don't want you to join us, just accept our fast on your behalf. You should stay as healthy and vibrant, as hopeful as you can."

And then, the next day, a second letter, this one from my brother in the Midwest. It's written on parchment, with a fountain pen, the lower half of the three-inch-wide paper torn. He gives some context for his own practice: "Many years ago, I fasted. Not on a regular basis, but several times. I have not fasted for well over a decade." This brother speaks of a "hunger in solidarity with you," of wanting to "focus that energy of hunger on a greater <u>Hunger</u>," of "fasting to channel my hunger." I think of a river, banks channeling its rushing water, focusing it, propelling it forward, directing it, harnessing that which cannot be contained.

This letter, too, is dated 17 March 2016. My brothers, it seems, both fast and write together, and this second letter includes a sentence almost identical to one in the first. "Prayer is such a mystery." It is. And he, too, writes of hope, of a "hope for a long-awaited breakthrough, for you both to create a new consciousness, soul, baby."

What strikes me most in the second letter is its passing reference to fasting as a "gesture that further confirms you are not alone." This is another thing the fast is showing me—the embodiment of prayer, a way to think of the movements of a body as a prayer in and of themselves. That the fast, that prayer, might be a *gesture* I find compelling: I tend to think of gestures as something a body *does*, but in this instance, it is a gesture of stillness, of silence, of nothing, of absence, an absence that mirrors this absence in the womb.

Here's how the prophet tells his own story. Or, rather, how the writer of the prophet's story tells it. I want to think about Jonah's story as crafted, want to think about the decisions this writer—a person I distinguish from Jonah-as-prophet, and him from Jonah-as-character (even if the three may be one)—has made in telling this story.

After Jonah has been told by the Lord to go "call out against" Nineveh for their wickedness, the writer writes this: "But Jonah rose to flee to Tarshish from the presence of the Lord. He went down to Joppa and found a ship going to Tarshish. So he paid the fare and went down into it, to go with them to Tarshish, away from the presence of the Lord."

These sentences make a chiasm, wherein the form mirrors itself by following an ABC . . . CBA pattern. Chiasm takes its name from, and visually imitates, the Greek letter *X*—pronounced *kai*—its mirrored arms pointing to a climax at its center. Though a popular form in antiquity, it was not antiquity's most popular form. Here are the same sentences, reformatted to show forth their chiasm.

A But Jonah rose to flee to Tarshish from the presence of the Lord.
  B He went down to Joppa
    C and found a ship
      X going to Tarshish.
    C So he paid the fare
  B and went down into it,
A to go with them to Tarshish, away from the presence of the Lord.

In the original Hebrew, chiasms appear in the repetitions of words and sentence structure, some of which carry across translation. The A-level repeats the phrase "to Tarshish from the presence of the Lord." The B-level has Jonah descending "down" into something, whether city or ship, foreshadowing his later descent into the whale and into the depths of the sea. The C-level shows Jonah's actions, and the chiasm's center reiterates that Jonah is "going to Tarshish," one of three times Tarshish is mentioned in the verse; as the chiasm's center, it stands in stark contrast to the A-level's "presence of the Lord."

The two locales are placed against each other. Tarshish was a coastal city in Spain, and Jonah's decision to flee there—to sail west across the Mediterranean to what was then the world's edge rather than trek northeast to Nineveh (modern day Mosul)—is foregrounded by sentences that not only advance the plot but also, through their structure, emphasize Jonah's rebellion. The sentences become a way of organizing Jonah's world, setting Jonah, the ship and her sailors, the cities of Tarshish and Joppa (and, by implication, Nineveh), and the presence of the Lord in relation amid and against each other.

I note how recursive these sentences are, circling back on themselves, repeating certain words, revisiting them in a new context each time they reappear. The sentences (and story) would read quite differently if written as this: "Jonah went to Joppa and boarded a ship bound for Tarshish to flee from the presence of the Lord." That rewrite has a linear, driving, forceful movement. Jonah and the presence of the Lord stand in opposition to each other, framing the bounds of the sentence and of the narrative. There's an efficiency in my rewrite, a directness that loses the original's meandering (yet deliberate) repetition.

The rewritten sentence suggests a writer in firm control of the narrative; the chiastic sentences have a writer returning to ideas again, trying to ferret out their significance. The prose is layered within the chiasm, the writer juggling multiple ideas at once, circling back to them, never letting them be. The writer of a chiasm can't just set aside a word. The form necessitates picking it back up again. The chiasm precludes cursory treatment, demanding a writer hold an idea in abeyance so as to return to it later.

After Jonah boards the ship bound for Tarshish, the story continues:

But the Lord hurled a great wind upon the sea, and there was a mighty tempest on the sea, so that the ship threatened to break up. Then the mariners were afraid, and each cried out to his god. And they hurled the cargo that was in the ship into the sea to lighten it for them. But Jonah had gone down into the inner part of the ship and had lain down and was fast asleep. So the captain came and said to him, "What do you mean, you sleeper? Arise, call out to your god! Perhaps the god will give a thought to us, that we may not perish."

And they said to one another, "Come, let us cast lots, that we may know on whose account this evil has come upon us." So they cast lots, and the lot fell on Jonah. Then they said to him, "Tell us on whose account this evil has come upon us. What is your occupation? And where do you come from? What is your country? And of what people are you?" And he said to them, "I am a Hebrew, and I fear the Lord, the God of heaven, who made the sea and the dry land." Then the men were exceedingly afraid and said to him, "What is this that you have done!" For the men knew that he was fleeing from the presence of the Lord, because he had told them.

Then they said to him, "What shall we do to you, that the sea may quiet down for us?" For the sea grew more and more tempestuous. He said to them, "Pick me up and hurl me into the sea; then the sea will quiet down for you, for I know it is because of me that this great tempest has come upon you." Nevertheless, the men rowed hard to get back to dry land, but they could not, for the sea grew more and more tempestuous against them. Therefore they called out to the Lord, "O Lord, let us not perish for this man's life, and lay not on us innocent blood, for you, O Lord, have done as it pleased you." So they picked up Jonah and hurled him into the sea, and the sea ceased from its raging. Then the men feared the Lord exceedingly, and they offered a sacrifice to the Lord and made vows.

And the Lord appointed a great fish to swallow up Jonah. And Jonah was in the belly of the fish three days and three nights.

This, too, is a chiasm. Here is the story again, flensed to the bones:

A The Lord provides a storm
  B The sailors become afraid and cry to their gods
    C The sailors throw cargo overboard
      D The captain calls to Jonah for help
        E The sailors try to save the ship by casting lots
          F The sailors question Jonah
            X Jonah makes his prophetic confession
          F The sailors question Jonah
        E The sailors try to save the ship by rowing
      D The sailors call on the Lord for help
    C The sailors throw Jonah overboard
  B The sailors fear the Lord, offer a sacrifice, and make vows
A The Lord provides a great fish

Ask someone who Jonah is, and I bet they say he's the guy who gets swallowed by a whale. I find that when I tell the story, I focus on the end, too, on the moment the Lord provides a great fish and Jonah is swallowed. When Bartley's tale is told, when people wonder whether Jonah's story is true, this is the scene that gets attention. It's the story's most dramatic part, the moment that gets retold again and again.

But the chiasm asks readers to look elsewhere—away from the whale and toward Jonah's prophetic confession—the structure highlighting moments other than the plot-driven finale. The story comes together as it works toward the chiasm's center only to then unravel itself, the second half negating the first, such that Jonah's being swallowed is hardly its focal point. Jonah, as a writer, directs my attention to how the mirrored events in the chiasm are related. In the A-level, the Lord offers up a storm and, later, a great fish. In the B-level, the sailors fear other gods and, later, the Lord. In the C-level, the sailors throw cargo overboard and, later, Jonah.

The pattern continues. In each instance, action is repeated and inverted, and in each repetition and inversion, the event is set in a new context, its relevance and meaning evolving. In the D-level, the captain's cries for help are juxtaposed against the sailors'. In the E-level are the sailors' various efforts to save themselves. In the F-level, the sailors grill Jonah, their second round of questions now informed by the centerpiece of the chiasm: Jonah's prophetic confession.

And what of that prophetic confession? Its placement in the chiasm's center stands against the Lord, who appears in the A-level. The two oppose each other, both in the plot and in the story's structure. The A-level emphasizes the providence and omnipotence of the Lord, set against the centerpiece of Jonah's seemingly freely given prophetic confession. And so, there's a tension here, a tension the chiasm calls all attention to, a tension its form perhaps encourages, even creates: Jonah, in his rebellion, still prophesies.

The *Oxford English Dictionary* defines *maw* as "the throat or gullet; the jaws or mouth of a voracious animal." When Ishmael and Queequeg attend Father Mapple's church before setting sail on the *Pequod*, congregants sing a hymn with this line: "I saw the opening maw of hell." I cannot help but think of medieval art depicting the gates of Hell as a whale's gaping mouth—the "Hellmouth"—sinners marching down the maw into the belly to burn forevermore. *Maw* appears (three times) in W. S. Merwin's translation of the fourteenth-century Jonah-poem "Patience." Michelle Obama uses it in her memoir: "By now, I knew something about the maw. We lived with the gaze upon us," as does Philip Hoare when retelling the story of a man swallowed by a whale: "In secret his fellow sailors must have wondered what it was like to be within the belly of the whale, to slither down its gullet like a whiting down a gannet's neck and into the nameless horror of the leviathan's maw." Of a sailor murdered and thrown overboard by pirates, Captain Ahab says, "for hours he fell into the deeper midnight of the insatiate maw."

One obsolete definition of maw is "the abdominal cavity as a whole; the belly," and yes, Jonah does find himself in the belly. Another definition, obsolete by the seventeenth century: "the womb."

This is why the whale's belly is so appealing, why Jonah's story is retold again and again and again. The belly is both tomb and womb.

What seemed certain death brings new life from the maw's uncomfortable, indeterminate, uncertain space.

Easter weekend, in the midst of our infertility, I receive a letter from a friend. I reread it now, years later, thinking about the maw. "This note will probably reach you on Saturday," he writes. (It did.) "In a way, I think that's appropriate. With all the challenges, loss, and disappointments you've faced in the last year, you're living in a 'Saturday' season of life, a season between faith and sight." He explains it's easy to overlook Holy Saturday, to move right from the sorrow of Good Friday to the celebration of Easter Sunday, altogether skipping over the uneasy time between the two, a time marked by doubt. Though he never uses the word, I read this letter saying we need to have spent time there, inside the maw, to fully grasp the absence in the tomb.

What did Jonah do there, in the belly of the whale? The Russian Orthodox Church teaches that he reached out with each arm to clasp a rib and stood, arms extended, head hanging, crucified there, and from that pose, he prayed. His prayer, as recounted by the writer of Jonah:

> And the Lord appointed a great fish to swallow up Jonah. And Jonah was in the belly of the fish three days and three nights.
>   Then Jonah prayed to the Lord his God from the belly of the fish, saying
>
>   "I called out to the Lord, out of my distress,
>   and he answered me;
>   Out of the belly of Sheol I cried,
>   and you heard my voice.
>   For you cast me into the deep,
>   into the heart of the seas,
>   and the flood surrounded me;
>   All your waves and your billows
>   passed over me.
>   Then I said, 'I am driven away
>   from your sight;

Yet I shall again look
    upon your holy temple.'
The waters closed in over me to take my life;
    the deep surrounded me;
Weeds were wrapped about my head
    at the roots of the mountains.
I went down to the land
    whose bars closed upon me forever;
Yet you brought up my life from the pit,
    O Lord my God.
When my life was fainting away,
    I remembered the Lord,
and my prayer came to you,
    into your holy temple.
Those who pay regard to vain idols
    forsake their hope of steadfast love.
But I with the voice of thanksgiving
    will sacrifice to you;
what I have vowed I will pay.
    Salvation belongs to the Lord!"

And the Lord spoke to the fish, and it vomited Jonah out upon the dry land.

There is a chiasm here. Note the progression from death to life:

  A The Lord commands the fish to swallow Jonah
    B Jonah prays a lament from Sheol
      C Jonah descends from the Lord
        X Jonah reaches the bottom of the sea
      C Jonah ascends from the pit
    B Jonah offers thanksgiving from the Lord's temple
  A The Lord commands the fish to vomit Jonah

The A-level holds the Lord's orchestration of the story, appointing a whale and directing its actions. The B-level carries Jonah's lament and thanksgiving, the latter inverting the former, as so Sheol and the Lord's temple. The C-level focuses on Jonah's descent and ascent with the Lord and the pit again set against each other, and the center reveals how deep Jonah has sunk. The chiasm enables Jonah to move from confession to thanksgiving. It allows him to rise from the depths of Sheol back to the temple of the Lord. It enables him to descend and then ascend, to be swallowed and then vomited back up. The whale's belly is a liminal space, both tomb and womb, and the chiasm makes possible this turn from death to life.

It's a turn highlighted by Jonah's verbs. Note that he prays in the past tense. From within the belly of the whale, Jonah says, "I *called* to the Lord, out of my distress, / and he *answered* me." Jonah could speak these words only from the other side of the chiasm's turn, from the temple of the Lord. His is a prayer of thanksgiving, one that recounts, with gratitude, having been saved from drowning. In his prayer, Jonah is not seeking deliverance. He's not asking to be freed from the whale. Within, he's already been rescued.

Every interaction with the fertility clinic is strained. The nurse with her plastic cup, the stack of *Playboy*s, the arrogant doctor who says, "I'll have you pregnant in three months."

I'm ushered into an office for a physical. My wife waits outside. I lower my pants, the doctor pushes aside my penis and cradles my testicles, lifting each up, inspecting one at a time, feeling for lumps, commenting on how he's seen cases where they fail to drop. "It's called cryptorchidism," he tells me, "from the Latin for 'hidden testicles.'" I look down and think, *Well, they've always been there.* Abnormalities, defects, mutations, impotency—his language grates as I wonder how it might apply to my own body, these words I do not get to choose but may need to learn to say.

He then proposes to "assess your virility" by testing my chromosomes. I had always thought I was a male, but this test would determine if I am man enough—literally, at the core of my DNA—to father a child. As my wife and I walk through this infertility, I'm finding things I thought I knew about myself to not be so simple. What does it mean—not relationally or socially or culturally, but in the most basic, biological, physical sense—to be a man? We can't answer this question just by looking at my genitals. My naked body is not enough.

In her essay "The Hvalsalen," Kathleen Jamie visits the University of Bergen's Natural History Museum, which houses a miscellany of whale skulls and bones as well as twenty-four complete skeletons dating to the nineteenth century. Suspended from the ceiling by chains and metal bars, the skeletons still drip oil. "Poor whales," Jamie laments, "don't they know when to stop? The same whale oil that greased the machines and lit the streets and parlours, the oil of soap and margarine. All that oil! Here they were, dead for a century, still giving out oil!"

Jamie finds herself at the Hvalsalen—Norwegian for Whale Hall— during its restoration. The oil and decades of dust have made the skeletons a mess. The bones will be cleaned neither with lasers nor dry ice but with ammonia, ethanol, toothbrush, toothpick, brush, sponge, and water. Jamie notes the irony: "The blue whale, awaiting the attention of the toothpick. Then, they'd have taken everything we could throw at them. The full gamut of human attention—from the exploding harpoon and flensing iron, to the soft sponge and the toothpick." Museum employees raise platforms to meet the whales at the ceiling, and together, floating above the ground, conservators and cetaceans interact intimately, delicately.

Early in her visit, Jamie encounters the blue whale, this paragraph one I come back to again and again, in my teaching, in my reading, in my writing, in my thinking about whales.

Of course, the blue whale was largest of all. I decided to walk under its full length, and count my steps. First, I walked under the smooth horizontal arch of the jaw, and its palate, where the baleen had once hung, sheets of age-browned bone. Then came the solid complications of the skull, now under the barrel of the rib cage, the ribs curving down, enclosing nothing but air. I kept walking, counting. As I passed the basking shark I surreptitiously touched its cold skin, rough as sandpaper. I passed a dolphin, small and lithe, and making for the door. Still the blue whale went on overhead. Above the basking shark hung a huge sunfish, an eerie-looking object hanging from a wire, more like a black moon with an eye. Still I walked on, counting until the spine ended. Fifty-seven paces. Less an animal, more a narrative. The ancient mariner.

I hear a Jonah in Jamie. The whale above her, she enters under the mouth and proceeds below the skull, between the arches of the ribs, along the vertebrae, toward the tip of the spine. Jonah in its belly, the whale becomes a narrative, its body storying Jamie past various deep-sea denizens. Still, Jamie walks on, she tells me, still walking, still counting. The whale continues above, Jamie caught within. She defines herself in relation to it; she knows her size in relation to it; she understands these other creatures in relation to it. The whale commands her as soon as she enters under its mouth, and she marvels at it.

Later, joining the conservators on the scaffolding, making their way past bones while cleaning the whales, Jamie more explicitly figures herself as Jonah. "You could sit within the blue whale and look back, following the spine with your eye." Jamie's enclosed there, within the body, within the whale, but she is at ease: "You got used to the scale, even to holding conversations in these surrounds. To sit within the creature's ribcage was like being in a very strange taxi, caught in traffic." This is the language of entrapment, but for Jamie's Jonah there's a familiarity within the whale, a casual comfort within these bones: "To save from bothering with ladders and trapdoors, to get across from one side of their platform to another, the conservators just crawled between the humpback's ribs into its chest cavity, then came stooping out of its belly, and carried on their way." They come and go as they please. When one worker finds a fractured bone, he simply "entered into the creature's belly" to examine the break. Cleaning these twenty-four whales' bones, the conservators dwell beside, underneath, inside them. Jamie has sat amid the whale's bones, stood under its jaws, peered through its ribs, held onto them. She has been within.

I read Jamie with Dan Albergotti's poem "Things to Do in the Belly of a Whale" in mind. That same familiarity Jamie has with the whale's bones I hear in Albergotti's narrator, and each time I read his poem, I come back to the same questions: *Who's speaking here? And who do I become if I take this speaker seriously?*

> Measure the walls. Count the ribs. Notch the long days.
> Look up for blue sky through the spout. Make small fires
> with the broken hulls of fishing boats. Practice smoke signals.
> Call old friends, and listen for echoes of distant voices.
> Organize your calendar. Dream of the beach. Look each way
> for the dim glow of light. Work on your reports. Review
> each of your life's ten million choices. Endure moments
> of self-loathing. Find the evidence of those before you.
> Destroy it. Try to be very quiet, and listen for the sound
> of gears and moving water. Listen for the sound of your heart.
> Be thankful that you are here, swallowed with all hope,
> where you can rest and wait. Be nostalgic. Think of all
> the things you did and could have done. Remember
> treading water in the center of the still night sea, your toes
> pointing again and again down, down into the black depths.

I read this poem one of three ways. The first is for the speaker to be someone who's never been in a whale. This speaker imagines all the things one *could* do there to bide one's time. The possibilities are endless, this speaker says.

The second reading has Jonah himself as the speaker, responding to the question everyone must ask with a litany of all the things he did in there. In this reading, Jonah reports, listing off his activities, one after another, accounting for his time.

And the third reading, too, has Jonah as its speaker, but his mode of address changes. Rather than reporting, he is guiding. Having himself escaped, he now speaks to someone caught within the whale currently, this Jonah offering advice to another Jonah. In this reading, Albergotti puts me in the belly of the whale.

Though I find myself settling on this third reading, it bothers me a bit. I don't want to turn the poem into a homily, Albergotti's Jonah doing nothing more than doling out advice to my Jonah. But the poem doesn't devolve into platitudes. As for what happens within that belly, Albergotti's Jonah begins, immediately, orienting himself. He measures, he counts, he notches, he looks up the blowhole. This is an effort to find himself, to assess his surroundings. After measurement, this Jonah makes a plan for his time in this new space: "Organize your calendar." Distracted—"Dream of the beach"—his mind wanders toward finding an exit: "Look each way / for the dim glow of light." Getting out not feasible, he turns (or perhaps succumbs) to the language of the cubicle: "Work on your reports."

At fifteen lines, the poem behaves like a sonnet, a turn coming at the ninth line with "Try to be very quiet." After the frenzy of activity in the poem's opening, the narrator is now calm, listening, thankful, hopeful, resting, waiting, nostalgic, thoughtful, remembering. This Jonah has resigned himself to being within the belly, and he is content there.

We decide we're done with doctors, and my sister-in-law suggests we see a naturopath. We sit on this idea two years, not yet ready to enter back into that space, those rooms, those discussions.

When we do, we find the naturopath less invasive than other doctors, but she, too, orders tests, lots of tests. A hysterosalpingogram— or, more colloquially, a blue dye test—a transvaginal ultrasound. We make trips to a lab every other day for a few weeks for blood draws. My wife charts. And from the data, we find more uncertainty. It's unclear whether our infertility rests with her or with me or with us both. This, too, we cannot discern.

Even so, I'm finding an intimacy with her body, and with my own, and ours together, that I'd not known before, an awareness of how our bodies regulate themselves, of how the various systems within a body work together and (at times) against each other, of what it takes to sustain a pregnancy, of how our own bodies might fit within the bodies of knowledge offered by science and medicine. We're learning to say new words—follicle, progesterone, HCG, luteal phase III defect, heart-shaped uterus, cervical mucus, corpus luteum—words we never before associated with the bedroom. These words have been ever present in our relationship, the words lurking there, unbidden, lying dormant, these words acting on our bodies in ways we didn't know long before we found ourselves within this situation where we now summon them. When I was a kid fantasizing about all the things a couple could do together, such words were never part of my vocabulary, never part of how I conceived of sex.

And so the sex changes. We are sitting at our kitchen table, a pile of cotton swabs next to a bottle of rubbing alcohol. I sterilize her leg, load up the vial, push the plunger just a bit so a single drop comes from the tip of the needle. I pinch her flesh. She puts her hand on my shoulder and looks away. The injections sting, she says, and make her leg heavy. Blood blooms from where I pull out the needle. I catch it with a tissue and put on a Band-Aid. We are here, together, on this Saturday.

Unless you have a professional interest, it's possible that the only
bodies you've been intimate with, have scrutinised, have been the
bodies of lovers or children. The act of unhurried, unmediated
examination has hitherto been an act of love.

—Kathleen Jamie
Findings

On 23 May 2017, at 5:00 p.m., Ranger Gonzales found a dead gray
whale floating at Twin Harbors State Park, south of Westport, near
Bonge Beach, the waves pushing it ashore.

It's not a rare occurrence, whales found on Washington's beaches.
Many are juvenile grays, emaciated, unable to make their long migration along the west coast. There's the occasional fin whale. In 2015, a
Baird's beaked whale; in 2018, a thirty-one-foot juvenile humpback
out on the peninsula. The Makah tribe claimed it and then feasted on
it during their annual fall festival.

I read of this gray in the *Seattle Times*, and I begin to wonder if
I might retrieve its skeleton for my university. I imagine bringing
students to it when teaching *Moby-Dick*, theologians bringing students when teaching Jonah. I imagine biologists referencing its pelvis
when teaching evolution, ecologists using the necropsy to discuss
conservation of our great whales. I imagine art students drawing the
intricate shadows cast by the bones' swoops and curves.

I call Kristin Wilkinson, the National Oceanic and Atmospheric
Administration's stranding coordinator for Washington and Oregon,
to see about obtaining permits. Whether dead or alive, whales are

federally protected, and though I'm expecting bureaucracy, the permit process is surprisingly easy. After a few phone calls and emails, I'm granted federal and state permission to flense a whale and retrieve its bones.

If a whale dies at sea—as orcas often do—and sinks, the carcass becomes a whale fall (what a beautiful term, the whale having fallen both literally and metaphorically), its body an immediate feast and its bones a home all sorts of deep-sea organisms will live in for decades. And if the whale washes ashore on a remote beach, authorities will leave it to rot, the stench of its flesh not bothering anyone, the "winds and currents strong enough to flense whales and scatter their bones." But if that whale washes ashore near people (like the humpback in 2016 at Seattle's Fauntleroy ferry terminal, or the gray on West Seattle's Arroyo Beach in 2010), it must be disposed of. The public complains.

So what do you do with, say, a forty-three-foot gray whale, some fifty thousand pounds, like the one washed ashore in Everett in 2019? Some are buried above the high tide line; some are pushed back to sea. (That one was towed to Camano Island.) Others have been towed out to McNeil Island in the lower Puget Sound. The island houses a penitentiary. At one time, it held Robert Franklin Stroud, "The Birdman of Alcatraz," but whale bones now litter its beaches. The state and the prison don't like the island being a dumping ground, so Wilkinson is always searching for other places to lay whales to rest. It's hard, since no landfills in Washington will accept a whale carcass.

She advises me to contact Rus Higley. Running the Marine Science and Technology Center, Higley has built two whale skeletons. I call him and tell him I've a whale and don't know how to proceed from here. Though he's never before met me, Higley wants to go to the beach as soon as we can. He's giddy.

My original plan is to retrieve the full skeleton. When I tell the university's facilities manager, he says, "I don't get to decide what you professors bring in here, but if you bring in a whale, I'll find a way to hang it." Over the next two days, Higley and I talk often. Each conversation is at least an hour. "We can borrow knives from Jessie," he says. "We'll need a sharpening stone. You'll want to wear rain gear. Be prepared to throw it all away—anything the oil touches will be rancid." He walks me through how we'll dispose of the blubber. "Do you have access to a backhoe?" He says we'll need a crew of fifteen or so and three trucks to haul the bones.

The logistics daunting, I decide to treat this whale as a test run. Higley can teach the process of retrieving, cleaning, and articulating just a handful of bones, and after this project we'll develop a plan for a full whale while we wait for another to wash ashore.

And so we assemble a crew, smaller than originally needed. Some are biologists—Katy (one of Higley's colleagues), Veronica (a volunteer from the nearby Westport Aquarium)—but the majority are not: Eric (my brother and a trumpet player), his friend Alan (a chemistry professor), Isaac (a fellow writing teacher from my university), and Krister (our photographer, an old friend). The eight of us will go to the whale Tuesday.

Over the weekend, I talk with park ranger Gary Vierra about how to best access the whale. He tells me that on Memorial Day a child climbed atop the carcass. The weak skin tore. The child fell inside. His mother called Vierra, furious the park would leave a dead whale on the beach. He asked the mother, "What kind of parent lets her kid climb on a dead whale?" Vierra then prohibits me from using any state park facilities for cleaning up. "The last time a whale was here," he tells me, "the necropsy team washed up in the beach bathroom. Whale oil clogged the drains. The bathroom stunk for months."

Later that afternoon, I come across a dead rat in my yard. Its chest has been rent, its intestines spilled across the cement. Something has picked at it, perhaps a neighbor cat, maybe an owl. I recoil and look for something to scoop it into the trash. But then I pause. If I can't bear to look at this rat, how will I manage the whale? I crouch down close, inspect the rat's insides, look at the blood matted on its fur, poke at it with a Popsicle stick, tease out what I think is the liver. Bugs swarm across its still body. My nose two inches from the rat, I inhale deep, trying to get a sense of how death smells.

I return inside to look up "flensing a whale." I need to see pictures, to know what will be awaiting me at the beach. The images churn my stomach—the blood, the bloated organs, the piles of flesh, the fat and muscle strewn about. I'm beginning to realize, in some part, what I am about to do. I am about to flense a whale, and as much as I abhor whaling, I am about to become part of that history. This shared act brings us together.

The word comes from the Danish *flense* and is found in the Norwegian as *flinsa, flunsa,* meaning to flay, or to tear off. The *Oxford English Dictionary* provides examples of its use, each from the nineteenth century, each in reference to whales. With an eight-point scale, the *OED* notes how often a word is used. *Flense* falls on level three, "words which occur between .01 and .1 times per million words in typical modern English usage." *Flense* is in the same category as nouns like *ebullition* and *merengue* and adjectives like *amortizable* and *prelapsarian.* It's less frequently used than *maw,* which is a level-four word. We use that as often as *rodeo* and *candlesticks.*

The first whale bone I held my brother found on a beach in Alaska. It's a vertebra, its processes intact and well-defined, pressed firm and smooth. Eleven inches wide and eight inches tall, the vertebra is a weathered gray and drops sand on the shelf where it now sits. I can see where the spinal cord once ran, where blood vessels once entered. I'm no scientist, but given its size and shape, and based on comparisons with other skeletons I've seen and photographed, I believe the bone is from a minke, a yearling perhaps, maybe eight to ten feet long, that vertebra all that's left of it.

In *The Sperm Whale Engineering Manual,* Lee Post keeps a chart titled "Sperm Whales around the World." He lists forty-one skeletons, eleven of them in the United States. One is in the Whalers Village, in Lahaina, Hawai'i. I saw it last year. The whale hangs under an awning in an upscale outdoor shopping center, a Lululemon and Tommy Bahama nearby. Though this particular whale washed ashore in Baja in 1967, its skeleton stands as a reminder of Hawai'i's history as a port for whaling ships to restock before heading to Japan, the Northwest, or Alaska.

The whale is in disrepair. It's been painted white, the paint is peeling, and a few teeth are missing. Its hips are missing too, as are a few chevrons, but I later see in archival photos that in its earliest articulation neither were present. There's a story behind those missing bones. Perhaps they were never retrieved.

While I photograph the skeleton, my wife and son playing under its jaw, I overhear a kid ask his sister if it's a dinosaur. Their parents don't know. There is no signage, so I intervene. "It's a sperm whale," I tell them. "Full grown it can hold its breath an hour and a half and dive a half-mile deep." The kids think this is pretty cool until they notice the ice cream shop across the way.

This is the whale whose flukes threw its body from the water with just a few thrusts, traveled this animal around the world, took it to the depths of the sea, chased down giant squid, crushed wooden whaling skiffs with a single strike—those flukes wielded by a powerful spine, that spine now inert. I count the ribs and flanges, slide my hands along the jaw, marvel at a sternum as large as my stove top, grip a tooth, wonder about the placement of the scapulae and fins, and my niece arrives. She looks up at the skeleton and asks, "Where's the whale?"

As our crew gathers in the parking lot, I offer a few words for what we're about to do. "People have been flensing whales for hundreds of years," I say. Krister takes a few pictures. "We used the oil for candles, lubricants, crayons, soaps, the bones and baleen for corsets and umbrellas, the flesh for animal feed." I feel compelled to speak. The moment and our differences in purpose—commercial versus educational—both need to be marked.

We load our gear and drive a mile up the beach. I've seen photos of this whale, its body twice as long as the Fish and Wildlife Ford next to it, the whale on its side, mouth open. But when we pull up, I see the beach has opened its own mouth to receive the whale. It's three-quarters buried. Even in death the whale hides itself. Birds jump across its flesh. The beach is doing our work ahead of us, the whale's skin thinned by the days, its blubber tender, its body returning to dust. When I email the park ranger, months later, to see what's left of the whale, he'll write back, "Whale is gone," the beach having finished swallowing the carcass.

New Yorker staff writer Kathryn Schulz says that loss—"entropy, mortality, extinction"—is the "usual order of things." I know this to be true. I have felt the profound grief of loss. So too, Wendell Berry writes of the "democracy of the dead," and this too I know. I've attended the funerals of grandparents, a cousin, classmates, church members, a student of mine. These, though, are clean, sanitized. Death is present but at a remove. The dead lay in their caskets clothed and wearing makeup, their cadavers full of formaldehyde, their eyes closed, their mouths too, their arms laid across the chest, a string of pearls on the wrist. There is no evidence of decay other than rigor mortis, which itself isn't apparent since we don't touch these bodies.

Not so with this whale. Though I know loss, though I know death, here Death shows itself. It comes with maggots pullulating over a swollen corpse, working their way in and out, crawling over the flukes. They writhe, laying eggs in crevices. A number of the whale's barnacles have torn off, circular scars left in their place. The remaining barnacles have erupted. Whale lice proliferate, crustaceans on a cetacean. On a live whale they congregate in areas protected from fast-moving water, like in the blowhole or genital slit, or under the flippers—but here they move about unchecked, feasting away. Some are the size of a pencil eraser, others a fifty-cent piece. They are a washed-out pink. I pry one off with my pocketknife, the lice's mandibles clinching to the whale's skin, tearing it away. The whale has single blonde hairs, stiff like a broom, sprouting here and there across its body, each one an inch or two long. I pluck one and put it in my pocket. Blood, pus, and other bodily fluids have spilled onto sand and whale, and they've together crusted over. In places the skin has pulled taught, in others it has burst, and elsewhere it's been sliced for the necropsy. Internal organs are athwart. What I see most, though, is black, a strong black reaching across body and spreading to beach, consuming all it touches.

But before I see all this, I smell it—from hundreds of yards away as we drive toward the whale. In a piece for the *Toronto Star* about recovering a blue whale skeleton, Kate Allen describes the smell as "an almost physical presence." That's an understatement. The smell is assaulting, brash, a mixture of death, rancid oil, brine, and fish. I'd brought a face mask and some Vicks VapoRub for my upper lip, some mint toothpaste, too, thinking that it might block the smell if I were to smear it across the inside of the mask. Neither works. The smell persists, the smell prevails.

To equate a smell with something else is a roundabout way of describing it: this smells like this other thing, which smells like this other thing. It's tautological, like when I go to the dictionary to find a definition and only find more words. And to say the whale smells *bad* focuses not on the smell itself but my reaction to it. I think of a moment in Philip Hoare's *The Whale*, a scene when he's in a boat trailing a sperm whale. Hoare's companion retrieves a "sliver of sloughed skin" from the water. It is "gossamer-thin," and Hoare lays it flat in his journal, hoping to retain the smell of the leviathan. He says it's "deeply male and musky, strangely sexual and arousing." I am not aroused. Something deep inside me is disgusted. Millions of years of evolutionary instinct say to me DO NOT GO NEAR THAT CORPSE. Days later I'll be in a garden, and a friend will smell mint, pick some, taste it, and offer it to me. I will eat the leaf, and I will again be repulsed by the scent of whale that will cling to my fingers for weeks.

Now, at my desk, I have a copy of the "Stranding and Necropsy Report" prepared by Cascadia Research Collective. The whale washed ashore at 46.8336 latitude, −124.1084 longitude. The whale is a female—no longer an *it* but a *she*—one to two years old, and she'd been dead three to five days when found. Her length is measured in centimeters. Useful, I assume, for their accuracy, though to measure such a large animal in such small units strikes me as funny. She's 940 cm—almost thirty-one feet. The report says this of her condition:

> Laying on back, partially buried in sand. Slightly bloated. Skin slough-ing on fluke edges and insertion, area of sloughed skin R side of head between eye and pec fin, extending up toward dorsum. R eye bulging. No rake marks seen. Some healed superficial scratches in skin on flanks and healing superficial scratches on sternal area. Healed propeller marks R flank, posterior to pec fin, 5 parallel lines, 8-18 cm long, each 11 cm apart.

The box next to "Boat Collision?" is checked, and there are notes offering more details under "Human Interaction":

> Not related to mortality—healed propeller marks on R flank, posterior to pec fin. Possible ship strike as cause of death, good body condition and evidence of internal trauma but unable to examine dorsal aspect. Live stranding also a possibility.

The report continues. The heart: "areas of bruising L ventricle." The lungs: "tissue completely disintegrated, only airways remain. Bronchials bruised and collapsed." The stomach: "empty." Intestines: "pushed up into thoracic cavity." The blubber: "moderately oily. Diffuse bruising from throat to end of rib cage (not full blubber depth—approx ½ depth, outermost layer)." There is hemorrhaging, hernia, and hematoma too, and the whale's internal organs are "fall-ing apart much more than typically seen in whales with this level of decomp—internal damage that sped up the process is suspected."

I read the report's use of "also a possibility" and "is suspected" as pointing to the cautious mind of a careful scientist, one working methodically to determine a cause of death. I welcome the candor in describing this whale's body. Earlier that year, I read this headline: "50-Foot Whale Dead after Encounter with Ship near Tacoma." An "encounter"? Why hedge words? Can we not name what happened? A ship hit that whale and it died.

Despite the necropsy's scientific precision, I note the intimacy in this document, its accounting of the whale's organs, her skin, her blubber, her wounds. Perhaps it is the detached tone of the prose, sentences purposeful and trim, that makes this intimacy read as invasive. "A wound marks the threshold between interior and exterior," Leslie Jamison writes, "It marks where a body has been penetrated. Wounds suggest that the skin has been opened—that privacy has been violated in the making of the wound, a rift in the skin, and by the act of peering into it." That's what this necropsy does—it peers into the whale, her skin riven, her body wounded by both propeller and scalpel. Through the necropsy, I'm seeing the inner life of this animal.

"Is there anything in particular you want to get today?" Higley asks as we walk the whale, back and forth, planning our morning. Higley's average height, bearded, wearing yellow hip waders and an orange T-shirt from Hawai'i, the sort you'd get at a tourist shop on the beach. He's got a pair of Oakleys and industrial rubber gloves that reach to his elbows.

The dean of sciences at my university wants me to retrieve the hips, if possible. A neat evolutionary relic, he says. I ask Higley where we can find them, since there are, obviously, no legs on a whale. "It's really rare, but occasionally a whale will be born with little stubs back there," Higley says. He then quizzes me. "How would you find the pelvis on any other mammal?" My first thought is by the legs, but, again, we have none here. "It's easy," Higley says, answering his own question, "Right by the genitals." Higley assigns Veronica and Alan to it, telling them to cut in on either side of the genital slit and feel around for the hips.

This is how Higley works, breaking us into small teams and assigning each to locate and retrieve certain bones. We have a crew working on the jaw, another on the flipper and scapula. Higley and I kneel where we think the longest ribs will be. He hands me a white-handled knife with an eight-inch blade. I am scared to cut into the flesh. Can you butcher out of love?

I slide the knife in up to the hilt. Blood and water pour from the new wound. The whale's skin is a half inch thick and looks and feels like neoprene. Under it, the blubber is a good nine inches. I make an incision a foot long. I make another at ninety degrees, and another, so that I now have three sides of a square. Grabbing the blubber, Higley pulls down and out as if peeling an orange, and I saw across the fourth side. We remove this block of flesh—it must weigh at least fifty pounds—cast it aside, and begin cutting another. The whale is not as stiff as I had imagined. High tide has kept her supple.

My hands, my forearms, my biceps are now inside her. I have whale on and inside my hip waders. I can hear my knife cutting and her gasses escaping. I think I can taste the whale, somehow—it seems the air is heavy with whale, perhaps from the oil? When I walk around the whale, the sand below me gurgles and jiggles; there is blubber and oil and blood pooling and settling beneath me, out of sight; through my feet I can feel decay.

Katy reaches into the whale up to her shoulder, fishing around, to see how much farther she has to go before she can free the scapula. Veronica—working not in hip waders but a purple shirt and jeans, apparently not concerned about getting whale on herself—has retrieved the hips. She pauses a moment, taking stock of the whale, then goes to work on a rib. Higley and I are trying to separate two vertebrae. Between them is a yogurt-like filling. I later learn it's mucoprotein gel.

I now know my naïveté. I'd thought we would just slice into the whale, grab a bone, and pull it out. The whale has taught me—in the most visceral way possible—that bones are attached to everything. They're clothed with muscles, tendons, ligaments, and sinews, and all this must be cut from bone and body. And try as I might, I just can't muster the same enthusiasm as these biologists. It's all I can do to keep working. Throughout the day vomit comes up my throat and then returns back again. When it does, I pause, sit up, and breathe the sea air. I'm thankful for the wind. Trying to be helpful, but needing distance from the whale, I take to sharpening knives. Covered in flesh and sand, they dull within a few minutes of work. Higley notices. "How do you like that, English professor?" he calls out when I back away. "A lot different than your books, huh?"

It is. I'm learning about the whale here in ways I never could have imagined. I see myself as reading this body—reading it as I would one of my books, the whale itself a library of sorts, an archive, even. Nick Pyenson writes that "whales carry many stories in their bodies." He's speaking of harpoons lodged in their blubber, pregnancy scars on their ovaries, proteins housed in their eyeballs, each artifact speaking to the whale's life, and I wonder what stories are carried in this body, in this whale here on this beach, this juvenile all but two years old. She was born in Baja, had returned there once, maybe twice, and was probably weaned within the last year. There is no plastic in her stomach. She appears well fed. No teeth marks from killer whales. But she's got those propeller wounds along her flanks, and all that internal decomposition and bruising—these stories, and others, housed within her.

After dragging one of her flippers across the beach and hoisting it into Higley's truck, I now know what *dead weight* means. New words are entering my vocabulary. Actually, they aren't new words at all, but old words from an old tradition. *Flense. Flay. Carcass. Corpse. Flesh. Rot.* I have never used these words in relation to whales, and I do not get to choose them. They've been given me. I am learning what it means to say them and what it means, too, to do the things that necessitate their saying.

Whale bones are full of oil and unless extracted it will drip out. I ask around of people who've built whale skeletons, and some boil their bones to remove the oil. To do that, I would need a very large tub, a lot of propane, and somewhere to dispose of the oily sludge produced when water and oil separate. Others sink their bones, letting saltwater pull out the oil. To do that, I'd need access to a secure and private cove. Still others leave their bones on a beach to weather until clean, but this runs the risk of bones stolen by animal or human.

While we work at the beach, Higley gives his recommendation: burial. Six months in horse manure will leach all the oil from the bones, he says, the worms, enzymes, and bacteria in the shit and the soil feeding on the whale's remains. Then, Higley tells me, we'll exhume the bones and move them to a roof to sit a year to be weathered by wind and rain, bleached by sun. This will kill any bacteria and leave them white, as we expect bones to be.

The Organic Gardening Club at my university has a plot of land on campus, and the club's supervisor gives me the okay to bury our bones there. He's a colleague from the biology department, and he and his four-year-old son dig the grave. It's two feet deep, eight feet long, four feet wide, waiting empty for us. "Digging a grave is one thing," Wendell Berry writes, speaking as a gravedigger in his novel *Jayber Crow*, but "filling a grave is another thing altogether." He continues:

> There is something just about unbearably intimate about filling a grave, especially if it matters to you whose grave it is. I would rather do it myself. I would rather, if I had my rathers, not be seen doing it. It is the very giving of the body to the earth, the sealing over of its absence until the world's end.

I remember walking with my dog one morning in Pittsburgh, through the Greenfield cemetery. Ahead of us, up the hill, silhouetted in fog, three members of the grounds crew—two with shovels, the third on a backhoe—were digging a grave. Soil steamed in the cool air. It was their job, yes, but I felt I was intruding on something private, these men preparing a place for the dead to rest, a place for a family to mourn.

The whale is on her left side, her body twisted so that the top of her head is on the beach, her throat facing the sky. I'm kneeling in her mouth, my knees on its roof, working on her right jaw. Next to me, against my thigh, is her tongue, some five hundred pounds Higley guesses.

I wedge my hands down toward the underside of her jaw. The bone is seven feet long, a foot wide. My brother and Higley and I heave it, torqueing the jaw so there is tension on the flesh holding it fast. Katy and Isaac move in with knives, cutting where they can see the strain.

The whale's insides are surprisingly cool. I'd expected otherwise, this whale having sat on the beach more than a week, her corpse baking in the sun, her oils slowly cooking, her insides fermenting. But as I reach inside cold envelops my hands. Against the wind and sun, against the sand blowing in my hair, her carcass is inviting.

Perhaps there are some things you can learn only when you are within. And here I am, pushing up against this whale's muscled flesh. Ishmael warns me of speaking too much about what it's like inside a whale—"have a care how you seize the privilege of Jonah alone"—but it seems that, sitting here, inside her mouth, I might now be in a place to say something. And from here, looking around at how tightly packed her ribcage is, internal organs scattered across the beach, I can't imagine how a man could ever fit within her belly.

It's not possible to be this close to a living whale. My hands and arms are inside her, her blood and fat and oil smeared across my skin. This moment at the beach is strangely intimate, not only for how sensual it is—all my senses are engaged here, in an overload I've never before experienced—but also because I've never been inside like this before, never been this close to another body aside from those that make up my most cherished relationships. Kathleen Jamie speaks to this intimacy, noting that the only bodies we scrutinize are the bodies of our children and lovers—that is, unless we are in some sort of professional capacity, like I am, this afternoon.

Months later, my friend tells me about a routine physical. When he laid his hands on his patient's stomach, the patient—a homeless man, his T-shirt folded on a nearby chair—jumped. My friend paused, wondering if he'd startled him. As he ran his hands along the patient's spine and then prodded his sides, the man flinched again. "I haven't had sex since 1983," he confessed. "No one has touched me since then."

That fall, the bones buried and their flesh decomposing, the school's Theology Department along with the Gardening Club holds a "Blessing of the Beds," a time to pray over the land and the upcoming harvest. I attend. The liturgy includes readings from the prophet Isaiah and the Gospel of St. Mark.

We're asked to find a place in the garden and pray for the land, both here and throughout the world, and for justice for those who work it. Walking through the garden, I remember an essay from Kathleen Jamie in which she tells of coming upon a dead whale on a beach. She is stunned by it, and she writes that "some gesture seemed required" to honor its life, its body. And in this moment, I remember, too, my great grandfather Hieronymus, a farmer in eastern Montana. Each morning he'd walk into his field, kneel, and pick up a handful of dirt. He'd sift the earth through his fingers, feeling its moisture as he'd pray over his land, the soil falling from his hands back to the ground.

This, then, is the gesture required. I kneel over my bones, take up the dirt, and grind it into my palms. "You, O God, are the Creator, Redeemer, and Sustainer of all creation," the pastor prays. We answer, "You are the maker of the mysteries of life: sun, rain, soil, and air."

I am coming to know this whale. I'd thought of names on the way to the beach, perhaps Eleanor (my wife's middle name), perhaps Grey. Higley tells me, "The only things we name are kids and pets, and a whale is neither." Naming suggests ownership, so Higley has never named any whale he's worked on. These whales, he says, should remain wild. Cascadia Research, in their necropsy, refers to the whale as CRC-1587, but for our purposes, the whale remains *the whale.*

And from the whale, we retrieve six ribs, one jawbone, one intact flipper, and one scapula, all these from the whale's right side, as well as both hips, three chevrons, two vertebrae, and one sheet of baleen. I see from the necropsy that others have been here before us. The Makah took some baleen and barnacles. Northwest ZooPath took the heart, the ovaries, the uterus, and samples from the propeller wound.

The bones we've extracted are heaped amid chunks of blubber, pieces of whale littered across the beach. Our photographer wants a picture of the crew, each holding a bone. We assemble, whale to our left, ocean behind us. I recall old photos of whalers, lined up as we are, though they stand atop their kill (or inside its mouth, if a bowhead whale). I am uneasy with our reproduction of that scene, holding these ribs, a few vertebrae at our feet, the jaw leaning against my shoulder as I wince into the sun. I wonder what I am doing at this beach, wonder how the day will be remembered by the crew, wonder how this story will be told and received.

The day coming to a close, I take a moment for myself, walking toward, and into, the ocean. I drop to my knees. The tide washes over me, its salt cleansing. I look around at a sheen of oil atop the water. The ocean is taking back the body of this whale, pulling hers from mine, the oil slicking from my hip waders and returning to the sea.

The bones are slippery from their gore. We wrap them in tarps like burritos, pile them in Higley's truck, and then begin washing up. To contain the smell, our photographer spreads some charcoal over the load, and, atop that, he dumps a few boxes of baking soda. It doesn't work.

"The last time I worked on a whale," Katy tells us as she takes off her windbreaker, "I touched my steering wheel before I'd washed my hands. It stunk for a year." I don't want to make this mistake, so when Higley gives directions I follow them word for word. I scrub my exposed skin with handfuls of sand, exfoliating everything I can. "Now, wash off twice with dish soap," he says, the dish soap (in theory) cutting the oil. I do. "Throw everything you're wearing into the trash." More good advice: the oil has penetrated my hip waders, my jeans beneath, and even my underwear, all of it greasy.

I want to take a hot shower. "Oh, don't do that," Higley warns. After the first whale he worked on, Higley too wanted a hot shower. "But you know what happens in a hot shower, right? Your pores open!" And so his did, absorbing the whale. He stunk for a month. Cold showers for a week, he advises, to sheet off the oil. I do as I am told. When I arrive home, my pregnant wife—she with a heightened sense of smell—buys lemons for her oily, briny, fishy husband, and I grind them over my fingernails daily. Despite the cold showers and lemons, for weeks she tells me she can smell whale.

After four hours of work, the bones extracted from the whale and stowed, our bodies relatively clean, we climb into the bed of Higley's truck, atop the bones. As we pull away from the carcass a cloud of birds descends. They begin feeding. This evening coyotes will come.

Eight months after the flensing I take my son to his first Ash Wednesday service. Purple paraments hang in a dark and silent sanctuary, candles lit. I say the words of the liturgy, and I hold my son, my long-awaited son for whom we, in our infertility, mourned and in whom we, through the mysteries of pregnancy, now rejoice. I walk down the aisle, my son asleep in my arms, his head resting on my shoulder. "From dust you came and to dust you shall return," the priest says, dipping his thumb in ash and imposing a cross on my forehead. He again dips his thumb in the ash and again intones the words, marking my son.

Jonah stirs. He's seven months old. I do not like remembering my own mortality, let alone his. The rain falls on us all, but I think of these bones I have, bones buried under a blanket of earth. Grass grows there again, and it's the deepest green I've ever seen.

On Advocacy

By some measures, it would seem whales are doing well in Washington. Humpbacks are returning to the area, and gray whales have reached historic levels. The whale I flensed in chapter 6—while certainly a sad event that it washed ashore dead—in a roundabout way testifies to the grays' recovery. As Higley told me, "They can't die here unless they're here."

And yet, as I was writing *Touching This Leviathan*, I found myself having to make again and again the same disconcerting edit. In chapter 2, I mention the seventy-two orcas that frequent the Puget Sound. These are the whales of J-, K-, and L-pods, collectively called the Southern Resident Killer Whales. In that chapter's first draft, written just a few years ago, there were eighty-three of them. Each time I worked on the chapter, I had to lower that number, one or two at time, the whales disappearing. I pray I won't, but before this book goes to press, I may have to edit that number again.

In 2016, between May 20 and August 10, the Southern Residents were sighted twenty-one days from Lime Kiln State Park. In 2017, during that same stretch, they were sighted eight days. In May 2018, when I made the visit to Lime Kiln that I write about in chapter 2, no orcas from J-, K-, and L-pod were seen in inland waters, the first such occurrence since researchers began tracking these whales in 1976. This is alarming; the Puget Sound is these orcas' neighborhood. They travel beyond the area, yes, but these waters are their home.

Their absence is but one data point on a years-long trend. The Southern Residents' diet is 80 percent salmon, and as the salmon stocks decline, the whales go elsewhere for food—if they can even find it. Populations of their preferred chinook are at 10 percent of historic levels. Since 2015, no calves born to these pods have survived. There's not enough food to sustain a pregnancy or nurture the young. And it's not just the lack of salmon that's a problem; there are compounding factors. Increasing boat traffic means increasing underwater noise, which means ever-increasing difficulty hunting and communicating. To the north there's talk of building an oil pipeline in British Columbia, which would mean even more boat traffic and the risk of a spill. There's already so much pollution in these waters—huge quantities highly concentrated in a killer whale's blubber—that when an orca washes ashore, its body is considered (and disposed of as) toxic waste.

Salmon, boats, noise, oil, pollution—complex problems do not have simple solutions. Consider the call to breach the four dams on the Lower Snake River. Doing so would increase salmon runs dramatically, bringing more food to the whales. It's likely their only chance for survival. But because of those (and other) dams, Washington produces more hydroelectric power than any other state. Must we then choose between clean energy and orcas? And what of the agriculture made possible by irrigation from the dams? Pitting the economy, clean energy, and orcas against one another is an impossible situation. The loss of any of them has dire consequences—especially the loss of an apex predator, which would devastate an already fragile ecosystem.

I've not tried to offer any answers here. *Touching This Leviathan* asks how we might come to know whales. It is not a book of natural history, nor a book with the latest research on conservation efforts, nor a guide for how we might save the whales. Others have carried out those projects, and mightily so. We would all do well to read their work and then act in response. I recommend Jason Colby's *Orca: How We Came to Know and Love the Ocean's Greatest Predator* for a robust history of killer whales in the northwest. Lynda V. Mapes's excellent "Hostile Waters: Orcas in Peril," a five-part series for the *Seattle Times*, is the best articulation of these issues as they currently stand. From there, look to Ken Balcomb's work at the Center for Whale Research for science-based advocacy and hope for tomorrow's whales.

Acknowledgments

When I pick up a book, any book, the first page I read is the acknowledgments. As a writer, I'm interested in the community that brings an idea to print. Next I move to the bibliography. It's a way to situate the book, to place a writer within a larger conversation, to gauge whether I know any of the people, and any of the things being said, in this parlor I'm about to enter.

One of the best acknowledgment pages I've read is in Robert Macfarlane's *The Old Ways: A Journey on Foot.* After the customary list of names, he closes with a page and a half on the introduction Henry James wrote to his revised edition of *The Golden Bowl.* James compares revising a book to following tracks left in a snowy field, the tracks evidence of a former self. Macfarlane notes that, for James, the person following these footsteps "does not leave, in the language of tracking, a 'clean register.'" There are new footprints bursting from the old, the snow broken afresh.

As Macfarlane puts it, "James sees our misprints—the false steps and 'disparities' that we make as we track—to be creative acts." Macfarlane then equates his own acknowledgments page to those tracks in the snow. He has "followed in the footsteps of many predecessors in terms of writing as well as of walking," and he closes with a "wish to acknowledge the earlier print-trails that have both shown me the way and provoked 'deviations and differences.'" Then comes the list, and a curious one at that: not a list of people he's cited (that's in his Notes), nor of friends, family, and colleagues (that came earlier in the acknowledgments), but of his favorite writers, poets, photographers, artists, composers, bands, and bloggers. These are his predecessors, each shaping his work in profound ways.

I notice, too, that Macfarlane frames this entire discussion around walking, around following trails. Fitting, as his book is about walking and following trails. But what strikes me most about this comparison between writing and walking is how *embodied* it is, and it calls to mind another

acknowledgments page, the one in Scott Reynolds Nelson's *Steel Drivin'*
Man: John Henry, The Untold Story of an American Legend. "Scholarly work,"
Nelson writes, "still relies on physical strength: eyes to pore over documents,
hands to sort materials into categories, and strong sitting muscles, what
historians call 'sitzfleisch.'" Having worked manual labor myself, I'm aware
the dangers of touting, too strongly, the physical demands of writing. The
comfort of the desk hardly compares to working a ten-hour day in weather.
And yet, very much so, the life of the mind is carried out through the body.
We are not "brains-on-a-stick" but embodied creatures, and writing certainly
is an embodied act—the writer's back hunched, face illuminated and eyes
strained by a screen, fingers dried and cut by paper, arms sore from carrying
bags of books, palms smeared with lead.

Nelson continues, still speaking about sitzfleisch: "But these are not my
strengths, they are the strengths of others, those who helped me. Many
hands, backs, and shoulders made this book possible." He then moves into
his acknowledgments and, like Macfarlane's, which reflect his book's concerns, so too Nelson's: hands, backs, and shoulders did the work that made
Nelson's possible, and as Nelson's book calls attention to the labor of black
men laying track in the south, it's appropriate he think through how others'
embodied labor bears on his own.

I'd long thought the acknowledgments page and bibliography distinct
genres until I read the acknowledgments to Stacey Waite's *Teaching Queer.*
Waite makes what seems a conventional move, thanking "those who are
willing to listen to your doubts, your worries, your crises of faith," Waite's
"those" here referring to her "closest friends." But two paragraphs later, Waite
thanks "the scholars (many of whom are quoted in this book) . . . who gave
me the courage to both argue for and enact the form this writing takes."
Gave me the courage. I can't help but read that line with her earlier "crises
of faith" in mind. It seems the scholarship, alongside her closest friends,
helped Waite through those crises. In this moment, the line between the
acknowledgments page and the bibliography blurs. When Waite also thanks
"the journals and presses that have published other work that was founda-
tional to [her own] book," here too the bibliography elbows its way into the
acknowledgments.

I pay close attention to Waite's merging the bibliography—which I too
often read as *Academy*—with the acknowledgments page—which I too
often read as *Home.* Waite troubles this distinction. Her life outside her
office shapes her work as much as those library books do. Waite brings the

two together, integrating them, attending to the writer as a whole person. I see that now, as I sit here writing my own acknowledgments at our kitchen table while my wife and son sleep, a table that serves multiple roles in our home, a black table stained with red and blue Crayola paint and with our names carved on its underside, a table that will soon be cleared of my books and computer and copies of earlier drafts and notebooks and Blackwings and whale books and miscellany articles so we can eat breakfast and, later, cleared again so our son can draw.

Maryanne Wolf also speaks to the personhood of a writer in her acknowledgments to *Proust and the Squid*, noting the dozen children born and eight people who passed in the seven years she wrote her book. Marking time by arrivals and departures points to a world outside the book, a world very much acting upon that book in ways conventional citation practices do not and cannot account for. A scholar's work is not self-contained. In the ten years I worked on this book, my son was born, six babies joined our family and closest friends, we mourned at six funerals, we made two cross-country moves, and we said good-bye to our much-loved dog.

These acknowledgments, then, speak to this book as a communal effort, the product of bodies, of following the tracks left by others and deviating from them, of conversations, of coffees, of trips to the pub, of walks, of emails, of letters, of long hours in the stacks—many of which made their way into the bibliography, the majority of which did not, their totality what made it possible to attempt to touch this leviathan.

I wasn't alone there in the belly of the whale. I thank the wonderful team at Oregon State University Press: acquisitions editor Kim Hogeland, generous readers Dan Beachy-Quick, Philip Hoare, and Elena Passarello; marketing manager Marty Brown; editorial, design, and production manager Micki Reaman; director Tom Booth; as well as copy editor Susan Campbell, and designer Erin Kirk. I thank the editors who each published some of my earlier essays, parts of which I revised into this book: Pat Donahue at *Reader: Essays in Reader-Oriented Theory, Criticism, and Pedagogy*; Summer Hess at *Out There Outdoors*; Patrick Madden and Joey Franklin at *Fourth Genre: Explorations in Nonfiction*; John Knapp at *Style*; Sam Otter at *Leviathan: A Journal of Melville Studies*; and Scott Slovic at *ISLE: Interdisciplinary Studies in Literature and Environment*. I've included these essays of mine in the works cited.

I thank Isaac Anderson, Kathleen Jamie, and Stacey Waite; together, their writing gave me a model to work from and helped me rethink what an essay might do. Noel Tague read my first bloated attempt to write the whale and told me I had three essays crammed into one. "Pull them apart," she said. I started tugging and now have a book in my hands. Mischa Willett read an early disjointed draft and responded, "The bricks need more mud," his feedback helping me figure out how to write braided essays. Thanks as well to Kennen Biornstad, Traynor Hansen, Rus Higley, Jennifer Maier, Grant Marstolf, Jeffrey Overstreet, and Jeremiah Webster for reading drafts of the chapters. Thanks again to Mischa Willett, Jeffrey Overstreet, Rus Higley, as well as Shannon and Matt Sigler, and Christy and Grant Martsolf, for providing opportunities to share drafts of the project with a live audience. Mark Read helped with the geography; Eric Long with the biology. I thank Andy Leuenberger for his letters and sending Anne Ridler's poetry, Brad Chappell for the knife, Milla Chappell for *If You Want to See a Whale*. Thank you to Peter Hopkins for my author photo and Dave Wittig for the cover photo. Thank you to Rus Higley for bringing me to the whale at Twin Harbors State Park.

Thank you to librarians Liz Gruchala-Gilbert and Carrie Fry for assistance gathering materials, and thank you to my colleagues at Seattle Pacific University's Faculty Writing Retreat and Faculty Writing Groups. Thank you, as well, to Margaret Brown and Jenn Wilson in SPU's Faculty Life Office for a Faculty Research and Scholarship Grant to support the writing of this book, and to Deans Rebekah Rice and Debra Sequeira for research funds. I also thank my students at the University of Pittsburgh and SPU, their smart reading of my work doing much to shape it.

One of my professors in graduate school, Paul Kameen, once wrote a book wherein, as he told me, "Every word was exactly where I wanted it." I took that as the bar for my book, and I thank Paul for reading a full draft and the rich email exchanges that followed.

My largest thanks to David Bartholomae. Thank you, Dave, for encouraging this book from its earliest stages and reading drafts along the way. I am deeply indebted to you, my teacher.

I thank my mom and dad for a childhood of books and music and teaching me to love each. I thank Eric and Aaron for being the kind of brothers who do the sort of thing that necessitates writing such letters.

I thank Quinn for our many walks when I worked through much of what would become this book. You are missed.

And thank you to Jonah and Jenna. This, and all, for you.

Notes

Even when the footnotes aren't there, there are footnotes.
> —David Bartholomae
> "Everything Was Going Quite Smoothly
> Until I Stumbled on a Footnote"

Touching This Leviathan asks how someone might attempt to know the unknowable, and one answer I offer is that knowing happens through how a person positions the self within a problem and within a discourse. This locative work happens when a writer engages others. It is often then documented through citation, location becoming quite literal as the citation pins quoted words to a page in both the new and the parent text.

In this book, though, I eschew footnotes, endnotes, and parenthetical citation. I do not want citation to govern the page. I hope the lack of in-text citations will lessen the seeming importance of a quotation's physical or digital location and instead move another kind of location—how one is positioned amid an ongoing conversation—to the fore. Such engagement is about more than finding a page reference: locating the self in relation to the unknown comes through language, through how a reader and a writer move about within sentences.

But those sentences are never our own. Hauerwas reminds me, "Theologians do not get to choose the words they use," and as I said in chapter 4, it's not just theologians he's talking to. We all inherit language, and we all have to then find ourselves within it by learning how to use it. Because a writer must use words handed down to make something new, citation necessarily becomes difficult, and, if I'm honest, I doubt it can ever be done fully.

I inherit words and put them to my own uses—quoting them, yes, but so too appropriating, rewriting, and resisting them—and so there are sentences throughout this book that are not, and could never be, cited. Even so, I'll make the good-faith effort. My citations (rather, those I know of) follow. But how does a writer cite words that have long been internalized, ways of reading, writing, thinking, listening, and speaking that have fused with the self, such that they are within one's very bones?

On Method

ONE } Knowing Beans

13	"Behold, I am . . ."	Job 40.4
13	"Can you draw out . . ."	Job 41.1
13	"To grope down . . ."	Melville 110
13	"What am I . . ."	Melville 110
14	"Can you put a rope . . ."	Job 41.2
14	"Will he make many . . ."	Job 41.3
14	"Will he make a covenant . . ."	Job 41.4
14	"Will you play with him . . ."	Job 41.5
14	"Will traders bargain . . ."	Job 41.6
14	"Can you fill his skin . . ."	Job 41.7
15	"Lay your hands . . ."	Job 41.8–10
15	"Is this the creature . . ."	Melville 269
15	"What shall I know . . ."	Thoreau 107
16	*"I'll remember this day forever"*	Macdonald 20, emphasis original
16	*"One day this will be me"*	Macdonald 20, emphasis original
17	"requires pulling data . . ."	Pyenson 24

TWO } From a Distance

18	"A window opening . . ."	Berry 34
18	"if you want to see a whale . . ."	Fogliano and Stead 1–8
18	"not-so-comfy chair . . ."	Fogliano and Stead 9
18	"keep both eyes on the sea . . ."	Fogliano and Stead 23–29
19	"It was as though . . ."	Jamie, *Sightlines* 82
19	"It was probably nothing, . . ."	Jamie, *Sightlines* 82
19	"That way your eye learns . . ."	Jamie, *Sightlines* 82
19	"it might seem . . ."	Melville 159
20	"a large wrinkled roll . . ."	Melville 158
21	"Early this morning, . . ."	Orca Network
25	"best not be . . ."	Melville 208
26	"I try to be patient . . ."	Waite 13
26	a network of hydrophones	Orcasound
27	"Whale-watching, . . ."	Jamie, *Findings* 186
27	"literature of pursuit"	Anderson 82
27	The Psalms "were texts . . ."	Anderson 82
27	"God in not extinct, . . ."	Anderson 82

27	"Even with a camera . . ."	Anderson 83
28	"No more the whale . . ."	Melville 44
28	"unwritten life"	Melville 110
28	"more apt to call . . ."	Whitehead 161, qtd. in Hoare 69
28	"If, by some magic . . ."	Scheffer 180
28	"in a whaler . . ."	Melville 182
28	"The world was wrong"	Dillard 16
28	"an odd thing happened"	Dillard 27
28	"we all hurried away"	Dillard 27–28
29	"But enough is enough"	Dillard 28
29	"One turns at last . . ."	Dillard 28
29	"From the depths of mystery, . . ."	Dillard 28
29	"The reason I'd come . . ."	Jamie, *Findings* 164

THREE } A Heap of Stones

43	"Whales, of course, . . ."	Beachy-Quick xiii
43	"announce the whatness . . ."	Klinkenborg 42
43	"This is a planet . . ."	Klinkenborg 42
43	"at hand"	Klinkenborg 42
43	"if you look . . ."	Klinkenborg 42
43	"Don't neglect such a rich . . ."	Klinkenborg 43
44	"Call me Ishmael"	Melville 16
44	"threadbare in coat, . . ."	Melville 6
44	"I see him now . . ."	Melville 6
44	"the pale Usher"	Melville 6
44	"ה, *Hebrew* . . ."	Melville 6
45	"I give the popular . . ."	Melville 115
45	"Where any name . . ."	Melville 115
45	For *Black Fish* . . .	Melville 115
45	"his peculiar horn . . ."	Melville 115
45	Some call it the *Hump Back* . . .	Melville 114
45	The *Fin-Back* . . .	Melville 113
45	The *Sperm Whale* . . .	Melville 112
45	"is indiscriminately designated . . ."	Melville 112
45	"brimstone"	Melville 114
45	"Of this whale little . . ."	Melville 114

45	"He has never yet . . ."	Melville 114
45	"We project our myths . . ."	Monson 85
46	"the merry whale, . . ."	Hoare 24
46	"from the Scandinavian . . ."	Hoare 26
46	"classified as *Physter* . . ."	Hoare 66
46	"Even Linnæus's name for it . . ."	Hoare 84
46	"so called because . . ."	Hoare 201
46	"propensity to hug . . ."	Hoare 205
46	"the urban whale"	Hoare 205
46	"Beluga, or belukhas . . ."	Hoare 269
46	"from the Old Norse, . . ."	Hoare 269
46	"Grey whales were called . . ."	Hoare 167
46	"moustached whales"	Hoare 26
47	"That in oceans swim . . ."	Hoare 31
47	"My response to a Timothy . . ."	Monson 85
48	"grey-headed whale"	Melville 251
48	"pepper and salt . . ."	Melville 251
48	"are named for their . . ."	Hoare 300
49	"a kind of whale"	Hoyt 12
49	"of or belonging . . ."	Hoyt 12
49	$1.13 per gallon . . . $.12 per gallon	Hegarty 51
50	diary of Annie Holmes Ricketson	Ricketson
50	"Sent home 344 sperm"	Starbuck 638–639
50	the *Acushnet*	Starbuck 376–377
50	years later she'll lose	Starbuck 424–425
50	"Stove by a whale . . ."	Starbuck 228–229
51	The *Swallow*	Hegarty 15
51	the *Monticello*	Starbuck 590–591
51	the *Ann Maria*	Starbuck 358–359
51	the *Mars*	Hegarty 26
51	"lost several . . ."	Starbuck 358–359
51	"returned in consequence . . ."	Starbuck 440–441
51	"Burned by natives . . ."	Starbuck 550–551
51	"the captain's wife, . . ."	Starbuck 628–629
51	The *Abram Barker*	Hegarty 29
51	The *Draco*	Hegarty 7
51	the *Petrel*	Hegarty 8
51	The *A. R. Tucker*	Hegarty 34

FOUR } An Inheritance

63	"Save me, O God! . . ."	Psalm 69.1
63	"All your breakers . . ."	Psalm 42.7
63	"With hammer, . . ."	S. Murphy vii, qtd. in Hauerwas *Hannah's Child* 37
63	"craft requiring years of training"	Hauerwas, *Hannah's Child* 37
64	"Theologians do not get . . ."	Hauerwas, *The Work* 115
64	"Because they do not . . ."	Hauerwas, *The Work* 115
64	"Writing a poem is not . . ."	Christle 120–121
64	"But long before . . ."	Giono 3
65	"When I was left . . ."	Giono 4
65	"I wrapped Plath's . . ."	Christle 97
65	"there was no . . ."	Melville 332
65	"the odd inches"	Melville 332
65	"wished the other parts . . ."	Melville 332
65	"what untattooed . . ."	Melville 332
66	"Then I said . . ."	Jonah 2.4
66	"I had said . . ."	Psalm 31.22
66	"But I, through . . ."	Psalm 5.7
67	"The waters closed . . ."	Jonah 2.5–6a
67	"I sink in the deep . . ."	Psalm 69.2
67	"The snares of death . . ."	Psalm 116.2
67	"a writer who borrowed . . ."	Parker 503
68	"would itself be . . ."	Parker 506
68	"Usufruct"	Olson 26
68	"It is by no means . . ."	Horth 572
68	"a wicked book"	Horth 573
68	"my 'Whale'"	Horth 567
68	"Shall I send . . ."	Horth 570
69	"Applied to any other . . ."	Melville 334
69	"Give me a . . ."	Melville 334
69	"To produce . . ."	Melville 334
69	Beachy-Quick advises against	Beachy-Quick xiii
70	1966 comic book	Cabrales and Padilla
70	Captain Ahab's wife	Naslund
70	twelve words	Wang and Wang
70	"There are some . . ."	Melville 272
71	"to be able to . . ."	Bartholomae, *Writing* 197
71	"I would, for example, . . ."	Bartholomae, *Writing* 197

79	"Now listen right good . . ."	The New Lost City Ramblers
80	"For just as Jonah . . ."	Matthew 12.40
80	"Jarvis, . . ."	*The Avengers*
80	"I knew a whale . . ."	Glancy 102
80	"Imagine the silence . . ."	Beachy-Quick 25
80	"The bones of sailors . . ."	Springsteen
80	"When I moved back . . ."	Orange 64
81	"The coroner's report . . ."	Snyder and Jock 13, emphasis original
81	"A wild rolling whale, . . ."	Merwin section 2, lines 3–6
81	"But at that very moment . . ."	Quinault Indian Nation
81	"Then, up from those . . ."	Duncan 12, emphasis original
81	"A great big enormous trout . . ."	Potter 23
82	"I once more dived . . ."	Melville 331
82	"To enter this gigantic body . . ."	Eliade 64, qtd. in Beachy-Quick 112
82	"He has swallowed . . ."	Jeremiah 51.34
82	"One of the lads . . ."	Davis 241
82	"Over this lip . . ."	Melville 254
82	"The next moment . . ."	Barcroft Animals
83	MARLIN: "We're in a whale . . ."	*Finding Nemo*
83	"I shall not go . . ."	Augustine 170
83	"With a lantern . . ."	Melville 252
83	"Are there some things . . ."	Berry 52
83	"But for me . . ."	Merton 10
83	"Sitting upright and riding . . ."	O'Connor 216
84	"The sperm whale . . ."	Beachy-Quick 206
84	"No other human . . ."	A. Moe 9, emphasis original
84	"But the whale rushed . . ."	Melville 202
84	JIMINY CRICKET: "Hey! . . ."	*Pinocchio*
84	"My God! poor Tashtego . . ."	Melville 260
85	"He had found himself . . ."	Kastner 145
85	"It was in Queen Anne's . . ."	Melville 254
85	"How heel over head . . ."	Emanuel 65
85	"Joseph cannot believe . . ."	Doerr 246–247
85	"Imagine, for the largest . . ."	Pyenson 145
86	"Its heart is so large . . ."	Beachy-Quick 141
86	"The biggest heart . . ."	Doyle, emphasis original

86	"But come out now, . . ."	Melville 252
86	"Two or three times . . ."	Jamie, *Sightlines* 115
86	"In his amazing bulk . . ."	Melville 267
86	"For the fact is . . ."	Orwell 177
87	"The whale's towering . . ."	Marlow
87	"It finally dawned . . ."	Fox 300
87	"For truly, . . ."	Melville 274
87	"Upon news of a whale . . ."	"A New Cure for Rheumatism," qtd. in Giggs 43
88	"In 1827 a blue whale . . ."	Hoare 245
88	"Projecting from the . . ."	Melville 25
88	"'Oh this has been . . .'"	Montgomery 78
88	"Jonah, Ezekiel, Daniel, . . ."	O'Connor 76
89	"Look down, we befeech . . ."	*The Book of Common Prayer*
89	"Was the great fish . . ."	Glancy 102
89	"He had come . . ."	Hauerwas, *Hannah's Child* 148
89	"Presently, Q'wäetí is forced . . ."	Andrade 45
89	"The whale was killed . . ."	Fox 299
90	"After manacling . . ."	Silverman 162
90	"Within the body . . ."	Beachy-Quick 113
90	"And the Lord spoke . . ."	Jonah 2.10

FIVE } Within

Chapter 5 is itself a chiasm, section by section, as follows:

A We learn of our infertility
  B There's a strange shared desire to be within the belly of a whale
    C I attempt to address infertility through fasting
      D The chiasm in Jonah 1 reveals a tension between God's will and Jonah's
        X The whale's belly is both tomb and womb
      D The chiasm in Jonah 2 enables both confession and thanksgiving
    C We attempt to address infertility through Western medicine
  B People in the belly of the whale somehow learn to be content there
A We begin treating our infertility

The A- and C-levels carry the infertility narrative. The B- and D-levels consider Jonah's and others' time within the belly of the whale. The centerpiece uses *maw* to bring this two-stranded chapter together, asking that each strand be read in light of the other.

93	"And Jonah was in the belly . . ."	Jonah 1.17
93	"an apparently sincere account . . ."	Kastner 145
93	"in one of the . . ."	Kastner 145
93	the one Deogratias sent	Augustine
93	"doubled up inside, . . ."	Kastner 145
94	"(1) The whale's . . ."	Kastner 145
94	"has gone out . . ."	R. Murphy 145
94	it must have been a sperm whale	Wilson 631–635
94	"cliché"	R. Murphy 190
94	"I am constrained to say . . ."	R. Murphy 190
94	"the *Star of the East* . . ."	R. Murphy 190
95	"I would not . . ."	R. Murphy 190
95	"One evidently by . . ."	Fox 298
95	"The incident was . . ."	Fox 298
95	"We hear from Edgartown, . . ."	*The Maſſachuſetts Gazette* 585
95	permanent teeth marks	Dolin 128
95	"*A Review of the preſent State* . . ."	*The Maſſachuſetts Gazette* 583
96	"the Rev. Mr. *Stevens* . . ."	*The Maſſachuſetts Gazette* 585
96	"Now, art thou . . ."	Melville 67
98	"call out against"	Jonah 1.2
98	"But Jonah rose to flee . . ."	Jonah 1.3
98	But Jonah rose to flee . . .	Chiasm adapted from Trible 129
100	"But the Lord hurled . . ."	Jonah 1.4–17
101	The Lord provides	Chiasm adapted from Ramey
102	"the throat or gullet . . ."	*OED* "maw"
102	"I saw the opening . . ."	Melville 44
102	(three times)	Merwin section 2, lines 6, 11, and 55
102	"By now, I knew . . ."	Obama 257
102	"in secret his fellow . . ."	Hoare 155
102	"for hours he fell . . ."	Melville 238
102	"the abdominal cavity . . ."	*OED* "maw"
102	"the womb"	*OED* "maw"
103	"And the Lord appointed . . ."	Jonah 1.17–2.10
104	The Lord commands	Chiasm adapted from Ramey

six } To Flense

Works Cited

Albergotti, Dan. "Things to Do in the Belly of the Whale." *The Boatloads*. BOA Editions, 2008.

Allen, Kate. "The Blue Whale Tale." *Toronto Star*, 8 March 2017. projects. thestar.com/rom-blue-whale.

Alter, Robert. *The Book of Psalms: A Translation with Commentary*. Norton, 2007.

Anderson, Isaac. "Lord God Bird." *Image* 72 (winter 2011–12): 81–91.

Andrade, Manuel J. *Quileute Texts*. Columbia University Press, 1931/AMS Press, 1969.

Anonymous Student. Paper written for University Colloquium 1000, Seattle Pacific University, Fall 2018.

Associated Press. "50-Foot Whale Dead after Encounter with a Ship near Tacoma." *Seattle Times*, 13 May 2017. seattletimes.com/ seattle-news/50-foot-whale-dead-after-encounter-with-ship-near-tacoma.

Augustine. "*102. Augustine gives greeting in the Lord to his most upright brother and fellow priest, Deogratias (c. 409)*." *Letters, Volume II (83–130)*. Translated by Sister Wilfrid Parsons, S.N.D., *Fathers of the Church*, vol. 18, 1953. Catholic University of America Press, 2008, pp. 148–177.

The Avengers. Directed by Joss Whedon, screenplay by Joss Whedon. Marvel Studios, 2012.

Barcroft Animals. "I Was Spat Out by a Whale." *Snapped in the Wild*. Produced by Martha Hewett, edited by Shiona Penrake. 7 March 2019. youtube.com/watch?v=ChcEb6mlEUo.

Bartholomae, David. "Everything Was Going Quite Smoothly until I Stumbled on a Footnote." *Writing on the Edge* 20, no. 1 (fall 2009): 73–84.

———. "Teacher Teacher: Composition, Rutgers, the 1970s." Rutgers University Distinguished Alumni Lecture, 11 October 2012. youtube.com

/watch?v=BZxwkdrlrLM. Published, with some revisions, in *Raritan* 36, no. 3 (winter 2017): 25–53.

———. *Writing on the Margins: Essays on Composition and Teaching.* Bedford/St. Martin's, 2005.

Beachy-Quick, Dan. *A Whaler's Dictionary.* Milkweed Editions, 2008.

Berry, Wendell. *Jayber Crow: The Life Story of Jayber Crow, Barber, of the Port William Membership, as Written by Himself: A Novel.* Counterpoint, 2000.

The Bible. English Standard Version. Crossway, 2016.

The Book of Common Prayer and Administration of the Sacraments and other Rites and Ceremonies of the Church, according to the Use of the Church of England: together with the Psalter of Psalms of David, Pointed as they are to be ſung or ſaid in Churches. Printed by John Baskerville, 1760–1762. justus.anglican.org/resources/bcp/1662/prayer_sea.pdf. See also Brian Cummings, editor. *The Book of Common Prayer: The Texts of 1549, 1559, and 1662.* Oxford University Press, 2011, p. 613.

Bradbury, Ray. *Fahrenheit 451.* 1953. Random House, 1982.

Cabrales, A., and G. Padilla. *MOBY DICK.* No. 3, Ediciones Joma, 27 July 1966.

Cairns, Scott. *Short Trip to the Edge: A Pilgrimage to Prayer.* Paraclete Press, 2016.

Cascadia Research Collective. "Stranding and Necropsy Report for: CRC-1587." 2017.

Center for Whale Research. "Orcas & Salmon." Center for Whale Research. whaleresearch.com/orcassalmon.

Christle, Heather. *The Crying Book.* Catapult, 2019.

Colby, Jason M. *Orca: How We Came to Know and Love the Ocean's Greatest Predator.* Oxford University Press, 2018.

Crew, Becky. "World's Rarest Whale Seen for First Time: Spade-Toothed Whale." *Scientific American,* 5 November 2012. blogs.scientificamerican.com/running-ponies/worlds-rarest-whale-seen-for-first-time-spade-toothed-whale.

Daley, Jason. "New Species of Beaked Whale Discovered in Alaska." *Smithsonian Magazine,* 28 July 2016. smithsonianmag.com/smart-news/new-species-whale-discovered-alaska-180959945.

Davis, Egerton Y., Jr. "Man in Whale." *Natural History* 56, no. 6 (June 1947): 241.

Dillard, Annie. "Total Eclipse." In *Teaching a Stone to Talk,* pp. 9–28. Harper and Row, 1982/HarperCollins, 1992.

Doerr, Anthony. "The Caretaker." *Paris Review* 159 (fall 2001): 236–270.

Dolin, Eric Jay. *Leviathan: The History of Whaling in America*. Norton, 2007.

Doyle, Brian. "Joyas Voladoras." *American Scholar* 73, no. 4 (autumn 2004): 25–27. theamericanscholar.org/joyas-volardores/#.XJpWgphKiUk.

Duncan, David James. *My Story as Told by Water: Confessions, Druidic Rants, Reflections, Bird-Watchings, Fish-Stalkings, Visions, Songs and Prayers Refracting Light, from Living Rivers, in the Age of the Industrial Dark*. Sierra Club Books, 2001.

Eliade, Mircea. *Rites and Symbols of Initiation: The Mysteries of Birth and Rebirth*. Translated from the French by Willard R. Trask. Harper and Row, 1958.

Emanuel, Lynn. "My Life." In *The Nerve of It: Poems New and Selected*, p. 65. University of Pittsburgh Press, 2015.

Finding Nemo. Directed by Andrew Stanton, screenplay by Andrew Stanton, Bob Peterson, and David Reynolds. Disney, 2003.

Fogliano, Julie, and Erin E. Stead. *If You Want to See a Whale*. Roaring Book Press, 2013.

Fox, Francis. *Sixty-Three Years of Engineering, Scientific and Social Work*. John Murray, 1924. archive.org/details/sixtythreeyearsooofoxf.

Giggs, Rebecca. *Fathoms: The World in the Whale*. Simon and Schuster, 2020.

Giono, Jean. *Melville: A Novel*. 1941. Translated from the French by Paul Eprile, introduction by Edmund White. New York Review of Books, 2017.

Glancy, Diane. "The Lord Spoke to the Fish." *Image* 88 (spring 2016): 102.

Harms, Craig A., Kerry Wischusen, and Leslie Burdett Hart. WhaleScale. Version 2.1. Apple App Store, 2017.

Hauerwas, Stanley. *Hannah's Child: A Theologian's Memoir*. 2010. With a new afterword. Eerdmans, 2012.

———. *The Work of Theology*. Eerdmans, 2015.

Hegarty, Reginald B. *Returns of Whaling Vessels Sailing from American Ports, 1876–1928: A Continuation of Alexander Starbuck's "History of the American Whale Fishery."* The Old Dartmouth Historical Society and Whaling Museum, Reynolds Printing, 1959.

Hoare, Philip. *The Whale: In Search of the Giants of the Deep*. HarperCollins, 2010.

Horth, Lynn, editor. *The Writings of Herman Melville: The Northwestern-Newberry Edition*, volume 14: *Correspondence*. In Melville, *Moby-Dick*, pp. 559–576. Northwestern University Press, 1993.

Hoyt, Erich. *Orca: The Whale Called Killer*. 1981. Firefly Books, 1990.

Jamie, Kathleen. *Findings*. Sort of Books, 2005.

——. *Sightlines*. Sort of Books, 2012.

Jamison, Leslie. *The Empathy Exams*. Graywolf Press, 2014.

Joyce, Christopher. "Mysterious Type of Killer Whale, Sought after for Years, Found in Southern Ocean." National Public Radio, 7 March 2019. npr.org/2019/03/07/701101633/new-whale-species.

Kastner, William. "Man in Whale." *Natural History* 56, no. 4 (April 1947): 145.

Kish, Matt. *Moby-Dick in Pictures: One Drawing for Every Page*. Tin House Books, 2011.

Klein, Jo Anne. "Meet the Narluga, Hybrid Son of a Narwhale Mom and a Beluga Whale Dad." *New York Times*, 20 June 2019. nytimes.com/2019/06/20/science/narwhal-beluga-hybrid-whale.html.

Klinkenborg, Verlyn. *Several Short Sentences about Writing*. Knopf, 2012.

Lockyer, Christina. "Body Weight of Some Species of Large Whales." *ICES Journal of Marine Science* 36, no. 3 (February 1976): 259–273.

Macdonald, Helen. *H Is for Hawk*. Grove Press, 2014.

Macfarlane, Robert. *The Old Ways: A Journey on Foot*. Penguin, 2012.

Marlow, Jeffrey. "A Whale's Afterlife." *New Yorker*, 18 February 2019. newyorker.com/science/elements/a-whales-afterlife.

The Maſſachuſetts Gazette, AND Boſton POST-BOY and THE ADVERTISER. No. 738, 14 October 1771. In *The Annotated Newspapers of Harbottle Dorr, Jr.*, pp. 583–586. Massachusetts Historical Society. masshist.org/dorr/volume/3/sequence/624.

Mapes, Lynda V. "Hostile Waters: Orcas in Peril." *Seattle Times*, 11 November 2018. seattletimes.com/seattle-news/environment/hostile-waters-orcas-killer-whale-puget-sound-washington-canada.

Melville, Herman. *Moby-Dick; or, The Whale*. 1851. 3rd Norton Critical Edition, edited by Hershel Parker. Norton, 2018.

Merton, Thomas. *The Sign of Jonas*. Harcourt, 1953.

Merwin, W. S., translator. "Patience: A West Midlands Poem of the Fourteenth Century." *American Poetry Review* 31, no. 4 (July/August 2002): 3–7.

Minasian, Stanley M., Kenneth C. Balcomb, and Larry Foster. *The World's Whales: The Complete Illustrated Guide*. Smithsonian, 1984.

Moe, Aaron. *Protean Poetics*. Broken Dimanche Press, 2015.

Moe, Peter Wayne. "Of Chiasms and Composition, or, The Whale, Part II." *Reader: Essays in Reader-Oriented Theory, Criticism, and Pedagogy* 65/66 (fall 2013/spring 2014): 88–107.

———. "To Flense." *Fourth Genre: Explorations in Nonfiction* 22, no. 2 (fall 2020): 35–48.

———. "Life after Death: How to Build a Whale." *Out There Outdoors*, June 2018, p. 44. outthereoutdoors.com/life-after-death-how-to-build-a-whale.

———. "Sounding the Depths of the Whale." *ISLE: Interdisciplinary Studies in Literature and Environment* 21, no. 4 (autumn 2014): 858–872.

———. "Of Tombs and Wombs, or, The Whale, Part III." *Leviathan: A Journal of Melville Studies* 17, no. 1 (March 2015): 41–60.

———. "Virginia Tufte's Sentences." *Style* 52, no. 4 (October 2018): 385–403.

Monson, Ander. *Vanishing Point: Not a Memoir*. Graywolf Press, 2010.

Montgomery, L. M. *Anne of Avonlea*. L. C. Page and Co., 1909.

Murphy, Robert Cushman. "Response to 'Man in Whale.'" *Natural History* 56, no. 4 (April 1947): 145, 190.

Murphy, Seamus. *Stone Mad*. 1966. Collins Press, 2007.

Naslund, Sena Jeter. *Ahab's Wife, or The Star Gazer, A Novel*. William Morrow, 1999.

Neiwert, David. *Of Orcas and Men: What Killer Whales Can Teach Us*. Overlook Press, 2015.

Nelson, Scott Reynolds. *Steel Drivin' Man: John Henry, The Untold Story of an American Legend*. Oxford University Press, 2006.

"A New Cure for Rheumatism." *New York Times*, 7 March 1896, p. 3.

The New Lost City Ramblers. "The Old Fish Song." *50 Years: Where Do You Come From? Where Do You Go?* Smithsonian Folkways, 2009.

Norris, Kathleen. *Amazing Grace: A Vocabulary of Faith*. Riverhead Books, 1998.

Obama, Michelle. *Becoming*. Penguin Random House, 2018.

Ocker, Ken. "Washington State to Let Whale Rot on Beach—No Dynamite Needed." *Seattle Times*, 26 May 2017. seattletimes.com/seattle-news/environment/washington-state-to-let-whale-rot-on-beach-no-dynamite-needed.

O'Connor, Flannery. *The Violent Bear It Away*. Farrar, Straus and Giroux, 1955.

OED (*Oxford English Dictionary Online*). "flense, v." Oxford University Press, March 2019.

———. "maw, n.1." Oxford University Press, March 2019.

Olson, Charles. *Call Me Ishmael*. Grove Press, 1947.

Orange, Tommy. *There There*. Vintage, 2018.

Orca Network. "Sightings Archive—May 18." *Orca Network Archives.* orcanetwork.org/Archives/index.php?categories_file=Sightings%20 Archive%20-%20May%2018.

Orcasound. "Listen for Whales." orcasound.net.

Orwell, George. "Inside the Whale." In *Inside the Whale and Other Essays,* pp. 131–188. Victor Gollancz, Ltd., 1940.

Parker, Herschel. "Melville's Reading and *Moby-Dick*: An Overview and a Bibliography." In Melville, *Moby-Dick,* pp. 501–510.

Pinocchio. Directed by Ben Sharpsteen and Hamilton Luske, screenplay by Ted Sears, Otto Englander, Webb Smith, William Cottrell, Joseph Sabo, Erdman Penner, and Aurelius Battaglia. Disney, 1940.

Poirier, Richard. *Robert Frost: The Work of Knowing.* 1977. Stanford University Press, 1990.

Post, Lee. *The Sperm Whale Engineering Manual, or, Building a Big Whale Skeleton, with a Gray Whale Skeleton Project Addendum.* Bone Building Books, vol. 2, 2004, 3rd edition, 2012.

———. *The Whale Building Book: A Step by Step Guide to Preparing and Assembling Medium-Sized Whale Skeletons.* Bone Building Books, vol. 3, 2005, 4th edition, 2017.

Potter, Beatrix. *The Tale of Mr. Jeremy Fisher.* 1906. Penguin, 2013.

Pyenson, Nick. *Spying on Whales: The Past, Present, and Future of Earth's Most Awesome Creatures.* Viking, 2018.

Quinault Indian Nation. "Kwatee and the Lake Monster." Email from Leilani Chubby, 8 May 2019. See also Ella E. Clark, "Kwatee and the Monster in Lake Quinault." In *Indian Legends of the Pacific Northwest,* pp. 64–65. 1953. 2nd printing, University of California Press, 2003.

Ramey, William D. "Literary Analysis of Jonah." *In the Beginning,* July 1997. inthebeginning.org/chiasmus/xfiles/xjonah.pdf.

Ricketson, Annie Holmes. *Mrs. Ricketson's Whaling Journal, 1871–1874.* Old Dartmouth Historical Society, 1958.

Ridler, Anne. "Choosing a Name." In *Collected Poems,* pp. 122–123. Carcanet Press, 1995.

Scheffer, Victor B. *The Year of the Whale.* Charles Scribner's Sons, 1969.

Schulz, Kathryn. "Losing Streak: Reflections on Two Seasons of Loss." *New Yorker,* 13 and 20 February 2017, pp. 66–75.

Silverman, Kenneth. *Houdini!!! The Career of Ehrich Weiss: American Self-Liberator, Europe's Eclipsing Sensation, World's Handcuff King & Prison Breaker.* HarperCollins, 1996.

Smith, James K. A. *You Are What You Love: The Spiritual Power of Habit.* Brazos Press, 2016.

Snyder, Scott, writer, and Jock, artist. "Hungry City." *Detective Comics*, DC Comics, no. 876, June 2011.

Springsteen, Bruce. "Swallowed Up (In the Belly of the Whale)." *Wrecking Ball.* Sony Legacy, 2012.

Starbuck, Alexander. *History of the American Whale Fishery.* 1878. Castle Books, 1989.

Thoreau, Henry David. *Walden.* 1854. *Walden, Civil Disobedience, and Other Writings.* 3rd edition, edited by William Rossi. Norton, 2008.

Trible, Phyllis. *Rhetorical Criticism: Context, Method, and the Book of Jonah.* Fortress Press, 1994.

Tufte, Virginia. *Artful Sentences: Style as Syntax.* Graphics Press, 2006.

Tufte, Virginia, with Garret Stewart. *Grammar as Style.* Holt, Rinehart and Winston, 1971.

———. *Grammar as Style: Exercises in Creativity.* Holt, Rinehart and Winston, 1971.

Waite, Stacey. *Teaching Queer: Radical Possibilities for Writing and Knowing.* University of Pittsburgh Press, 2017.

Wang, Jack, and Holman Wang. *Herman Melville's Moby Dick. Cozy Classics.* Chronicle Books, 2012.

Weintraub, Karen. "An Elusive Whale Is Found All around the World." *New York Times*, 22 March 2019. nytimes.com/2019/03/22/science/omuras-whales-habitat.html.

Whitehead, Hal. *Sperm Whales: Social Evolution in the Ocean.* University of Chicago Press, 2003.

Wilson, Ambrose John. "The Sign of the Prophet Jonah and Its Modern Confirmations." *Princeton Theological Review* 25, no. 4 (October 1927): 630–642.

Wolf, Maryanne. *Proust and the Squid: The Story and Science of the Reading Brain.* Harper, 2007.

Yong, Ed. "The Blue Whale's Heart Beats at Extremes." *The Atlantic*, 25 November 2019. theatlantic.com/science/archive/2019/11/diving-blue-whales-heart-beats-very-very-slowly/602557.

A NOTE ON TYPE

This book is set in Warnock, an old-style typeface
designed by Robert Slimbach, commissioned by
Chris Warnock in honor of his father, John Warnock,
one of the co-founders of Adobe. Warnock's crisp,
eclectic features and practical proportions enable it to
perform well both on screen and in modern printing.
The triangular serifs give the type a chiseled appearance
with a mix of calligraphic and constructed shapes,
including both angular and rounded elements.